The Fatall Dowry: a tragedy [in five acts and in verse].
Written by P[hilip] M[assinger] and N[athaniel] F[ield].

P. and F. (N.) M., N F., Nathaniel Field

The Fatall Dowry: a tragedy [in five acts and in verse]. Written by P[hilip] M[assinger] and N[athaniel] F[ield].
M., P. and F. (N.)
British Library, Historical Print Editions
British Library
1632.
4°.
Ashley1121.

The BiblioLife Network

This project was made possible in part by the BiblioLife Network (BLN), a project aimed at addressing some of the huge challenges facing book preservationists around the world. The BLN includes libraries, library networks, archives, subject matter experts, online communities and library service providers. We believe every book ever published should be available as a high-quality print reproduction; printed on-demand anywhere in the world. This insures the ongoing accessibility of the content and helps generate sustainable revenue for the libraries and organizations that work to preserve these important materials.

The following book is in the "public domain" and represents an authentic reproduction of the text as printed by the original publisher. While we have attempted to accurately maintain the integrity of the original work, there are sometimes problems with the original book or micro-film from which the books were digitized. This can result in minor errors in reproduction. Possible imperfections include missing and blurred pages, poor pictures, markings and other reproduction issues beyond our control. Because this work is culturally important, we have made it available as part of our commitment to protecting, preserving, and promoting the world's literature.

GUIDE TO FOLD-OUTS, MAPS and OVERSIZED IMAGES

In an online database, page images do not need to conform to the size restrictions found in a printed book. When converting these images back into a printed bound book, the page sizes are standardized in ways that maintain the detail of the original. For large images, such as fold-out maps, the original page image is split into two or more pages.

Guidelines used to determine the split of oversize pages:

- Some images are split vertically; large images require vertical and horizontal splits.
- For horizontal splits, the content is split left to right.
- For vertical splits, the content is split from top to bottom.
- For both vertical and horizontal splits, the image is processed from top left to bottom right.

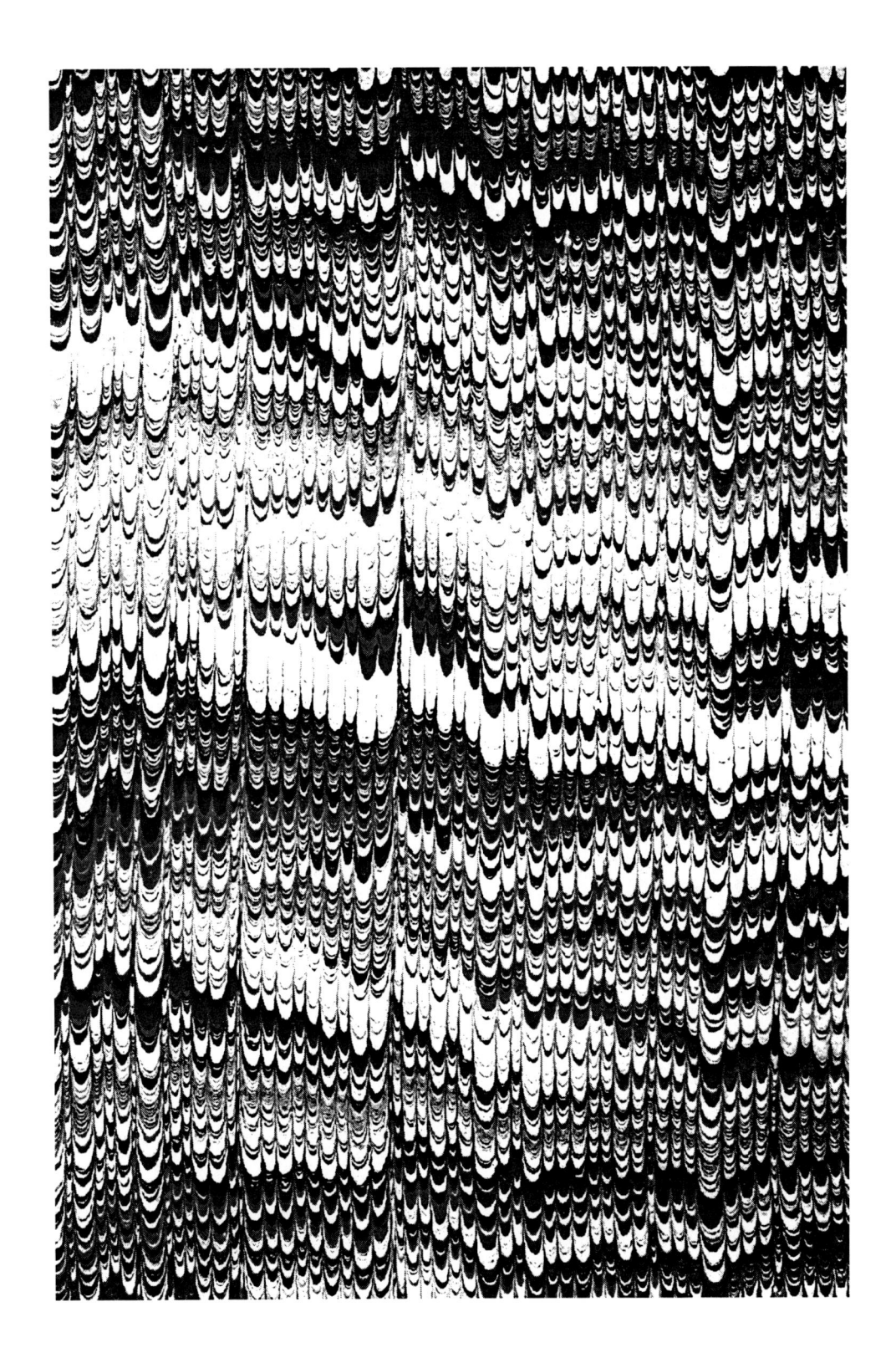

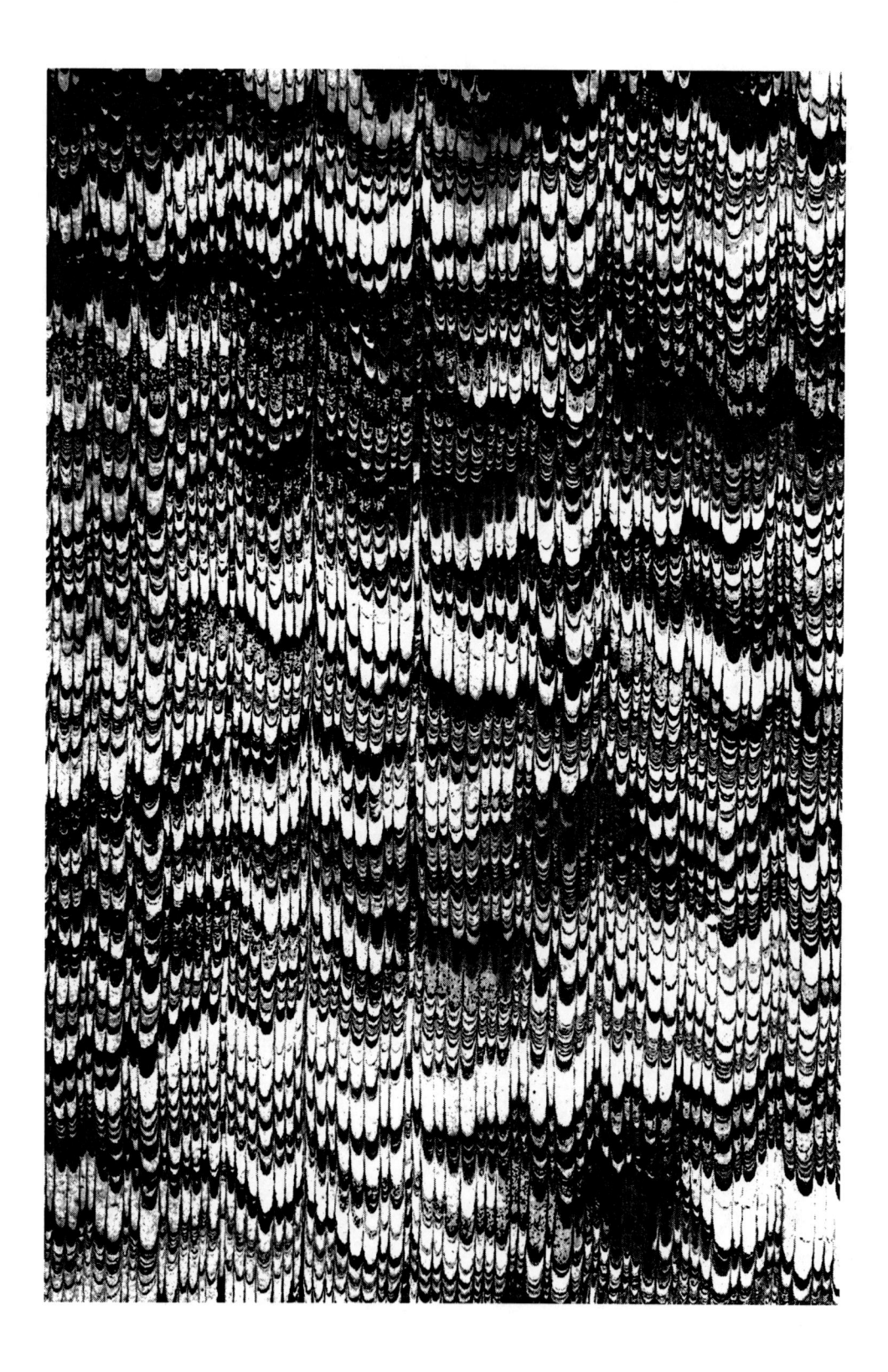

644. e. 85

THE
FATALL
DOVVRY:
A
TRAGEDY:

As it hath beene often Acted at the Private House in Blackefryers, by his Maiesties Seruants.

Written by P. M. and N. F.

LONDON,
Printed by IOHN NORTON, for FRANCIS CONSTABLE, and are to be sold at his shop at the *Crane,* in *Pauls* Church-yard. 1632.

Charalois.	Florimel. }
Romont.	Bellapert. }
Charmi.	Aymer.
Nouall Sen.	Nouall Iun.
Liladam.	Aduocates.
Du Croy.	Creditors 3.
Rochfort.	Officers.
Baumont.	Priest.
Pontalier.	Taylor.
Malotin.	Barber.
Beaumelle.	Perfumer.

First Song.

Fie, ceafe to wonder,
Though you heare *Orpheus* with his Iuory Lute,
  Moue Trees and Rockes,
Charme Buls, Beares, and men more fauage to be mute,
Weake foolifh finger, here is one,
Would haue transform'd thy felfe, to ftone.

Second Song.
A Dialogue betweene *Nouall*, and *Beaumelle*.

Man.
SEt *Phœbus*, fet, a fayrer funne doth rife,
  From the bright Radience of my M^{ris.} eyes then euer
I dare not looke, each haire a golden line, (thou begat'ft
  Each word a hooke,
The more I ftriue, the more ftill I am tooke.
Wom.
Fayre feruant, come, the day thefe eyes doe lend
To warme thy blood, thou doeft fo vainely fpend.
          Come ftrangled breath.

Man.
What noate fo fweet as this,
That calles the fpirits to a further bliffe?
Wom.
Yet this out-fauours wine, and this Perfume.
Man.
Let's die, I languifh, I confume.

Cittizens Song of the Courtier.

Courtier, if thou needs wilt wiue,
From this lesson learne to thriue.
If thou match a Lady, that passes thee in birth and (state,
Let her curious garments be
Twice aboue thine owne degree;
This will draw great eyes vpon her,
Get her seruants and thee honour.

Courtiers Song of the Citizen.

Poore Citizen, if thou wilt be
A happy husband, learne of me;
To set thy wife first in thy shop, (vp.
A faire wife, a kinde wife, a sweet wife, sets a poore man
What though thy shelues be ne're so bare:
A woman still is currant ware:
Each man will cheapen, foe, and friend,
But whilst thou art at tother end,
What ere thou seest, or what dost heare,
Foole, haue no eye to, nor an eare;
And after supper for her sake,
When thou hast fed, snort, though thou wake:
What though the Gallants call thee mome?
Yet with thy lanthorne light her home:
Then looke into the towne and tell,
If no such Tradesmen there doe dwell.

The Fatall Dowry:
A Tragedy.

Act. primus.   Scæna prima.

Enter Charaloyes *with a paper,* Romont, Charmi.

Charmi.

SIR, I may moue the Court to serue your will,
But therein shall both wrong you and my selfe.
  Rom. Why thinke you so sir?
  Charmi. 'Cause I am familiar
With what will be their answere: they will say,
Tis against law, and argue me of Ignorance
For offering them the motion.
  Rom. You know not, Sir,
How in this cause they may dispence with Law,
And therefore frame not you their answere for them,
But doe your parts.
  Charmi. I loue the cause so well,
As I could runne, the hazard of a checke for't.
  Rom. From whom?

The Fatall Dowry.

Charmi. Some of the bench, that watch to giue it,
More then to doe the office that they sit for:
But giue me (sir) my fee.
  Rom. Now you are Noble.
  Charmi. I shall deserue this better yet, in giuing
My Lord some counsell, (if he please to heare it)
Then I shall doe with pleading.
  Rom. What may it be, sir?
  Charmi. That it would please his Lordship, as the Presi- (dents,
And Counsaylors of Court come by, to stand
Heere, and but shew your selfe, and to some one
Or two, make his request: there is a minute
When a mans presence speakes in his owne cause,
More then the tongues of twenty aduocates.
  Rom. I haue vrg'd that.

  Enter Rochfort: *Du Croye.*

  Charmi. Their Lordships here are comming,
I must goe get me a place, you'l finde me in Court,
And at your seruice.   *Exit Charmi.*
  Rom. Now put on your Spirits.
  Du Croy. The ease that you prepare your selfe, my Lord,
In giuing vp the place you hold in Court,
Will proue (I feare) a trouble in the State,
And that no slight one.
  Roch. Pray you sir, no more.
  Rom. Now sir, lose not this offerd meanes: their lookes
Fixt on you, with a pittying earnestnesse,
Inuite you to demand their furtherance
To your good purpose.——This such a dulnesse
So foolish and vntimely as——
  Du. Croy. You know him.
  Roch. I doe, and much lament the sudden fall
Of his braue house. It is young *Charloyes.*
Sonne to the Marshall, from whom he inherits
His fame and vertues onely.
  Rom. Ha, hey name you.
  Du. Croye. His father died in prison two daies since.
                                   Roch.

The Fatall Dowry.

Roch. Yes, to the shame of this vngratefull State,
That such a Master in the art of warre,
So noble, and so highly meriting,
From this forgetfull Country, should, for want
Of meanes to satisfie his creditors,
The summes he tooke vp for the generall good,
Meet with an end so infamous.

Rom. Dare you euer hope for like oportunity?

Du Croye. My good Lord!

Roch. My wish bring comfort to you.

Du Croye. The time calls vs.

Roch. Good morrow Colonell.

Exeunt Roch. Du Croye.

Rom. This obstinate spleene,
You thinke becomes your sorrow, and sorts wel
With your blacke suits: but grant me wit, or iudgement,
And by the freedome of an honest man,
And a true friend to boote, I sweare 'tis shamefull.
And therefore flatter not your selfe with hope,
Your sable habit, with the hat and cloake,
No though the ribons helpe, haue power to worke 'em
To what you would: for those that had no eyes,
To see the great acts of your father, will not,
From any fashion sorrow can put on,
Bee taught to know their duties.

Char. If they will not,
They are too old to learne, and I too young
To giue them counsell, since if they partake
The vnderstanding, and the hearts of men,
They will preuent my words and teares: if not,
What can perswasion, though made eloquent
With griefe, worke vpon such as haue chang'd natures
With the most sauage beast? Blest, blest be euer
The memory of that happy age, when iustice
Had no gards to keepe off wrongd innocence,
From flying to her succours, and in that
Assurance of redresse: where now (*Roment*)

B 2

The

The Fatall Dowry,

The damnd, with more ease may ascend from Hell,
Then we ariue at her. One Cerberus there
Forbids the passage, in our Courts a thousand,
As lowd, and fertyle headed, and the Client
That wants the sops, to fill their rauenous throats,
Must hope for no accesse: why should I then
Attempt impossibilities: you friend, being
Too well acquainted with my dearth of meanes,
To make my entrance that way?

  Rom. Would I were not.
But Sir, you haue a cause, a cause so iust,
Of such necessitie, not to be deferd,
As would compell a mayde, whose foot was neuer
Set ore her fathers threshold, nor within
The house where she was borne, euer spake word,
Which was not vshered with pure virgin blushes,
To drowne the tempest of a pleaders tongue,
And force corruption to giue backe the hire
It tooke against her: let examples moue you.
You see great men in birth, esteeme and fortune,
Rather then lose a scruple of their right,
Fawne basely vpon such, whose gownes put off,
They would disdaine for Seruants.

  Char. And to these can I become a suytor?

  Rom. Without losse,
Would you consider, that to gaine their fauors,
Our chastest dames put off their modesties,
Soldiers forget their honors, vsurers
Make sacrifice of Gold, poets of wit,
And men religious, part with fame, and goodnesse?
Be therfore wonne to vse the meanes, that may
Aduance your pious ends.

  Char. You shall orecome.

  Rom. And you receiue the glory, pray you now practise.
'Tis well.   *Enter Old Nouall, Liladam,*

  Char. Not looke on me!   *& 3 Creditors.*

  Rom. You must haue patience ——— Offer't againe.

                                              Char,

The Fatall Dowry.

Char. And be againe contemn'd?
Nov. I know whats to be done.
　1 Cred. And that your Lordship
Will pleafe to do your knowledge, we offer, firft
Our thankefull hearts heere, as a bounteous earneft
To what we will adde
　Nov. One word more of this
I am your enemie. Am I a man
Your bribes can worke on? ha?
　Lilad. Friends, you miftake
The way to winne my Lord, he muft not heare this,
But I, as one in fauour, in his fight,
May harken to you for my profit. Sir,
I pray heare em.
　Nov. Tis well.
　Lilad. Obferue him now.
　Nov. Your caufe being good, and your proceedings fo,
Without corruption ; I am your friend,
Speake your defires.
　2 Cred. Oh, they are charitable,
The Marfhall ftood ingag'd vnto vs three,
Two hundred thoufand crownes, which by his death
We are defeated of. For which great loffe
We ayme at nothing but his rotten flefh,
Nor is that cruelty.
　1 Cred. I haue a fonne,
That talkes of nothing but of Gunnes and Armors,
And fweares hee'll be a foldier, tis an humor
I would diuert him from , and I am told
That if I minifter to him in his drinke
Powder, made of this banquerout Marfhalls bones,
Prouided that the carcafe rot aboue ground,
'T will cure his foolifh frenfie.
　Nov. You fhew in it
A fathers care. I haue a fonne my felfe,
A fafhionable Gentleman and a peacefull :

B 3　　　　　　　　　　　　　　And

The Fatall Dowry.

And but I am assur'd he's not so giuen,
He should take of it too. Sir, what are you?

   Char. A Gentleman.

   Nou. So are many that rake dunghills.
If you haue any suit, moue it in Court.
I take no papers in corners.

   Rom. Yes as the matter may be carried, and hereby
To mannage the conuayance —— Follow him.

   Lil. You are rude. I say, he shall not passe.   *Exit Nouall.*

   Rom. You say so.   *Char: and Aduocates.*
On what assurance?
For the well cutting of his Lordships cornes,
Picking his toes, or any office else
Neerer to basenesse!

   Lil. Looke vpon mee better,
Are these the ensignes of so coorse a fellow?
Be well aduis'd.

   Rom. Out, rogue, do not I know,   (*Kicks him*)
These glorious weedes spring from the sordid dunghill
Of thy officious basenesse? wert thou worthy
Of any thing from me, but my contempt,
I would do more then this, more, you Court-spider.

   Lil. But that this man is lawlesse; he should find
that I am valiant.

   1 *Cred.* If your eares are fast,
Tis nothing. Whats a blow or two? as much——

   2 *Cred.* These chastisements, as vsefull are as frequent
To such as would grow rich.

   Rom. Are they so Rascals? I wil be-friend you then.

   1 *Cred.* Beare witnesse, Sirs.

   Lil. Trueth, I haue borne my part already, friends.
In the Court you shall haue more.   *Exit.*

   Rom. I know you for
The worst of spirits, that striue to rob the tombes
Of what is their inheritance, from the dead.
For vsurers, bred by a riotous peace:
That hold the Charter of your wealth & freedome,

                        By

The Fatall Dowry.

By being Knaues and Cuckolds that ne're prayd,
But when you feare the rich heires will grow wise,
To keepe their Lands out of your parchment toyles;
And then, the Diuell your father's cald vpon,
To inuent some wayes of *Luxury* ne're thought on.
Be gone, and quickly, or Ile leaue no roome
Vpon your forhead for your hornes to sprowt on,
Without a murmure, or I will vndoe you;
For I will beate you honest.

   1 *Cred.* Thrift forbid.
We will beare this, rather then hazard that. *Ex: Creditor.*
           Enter Charloyes.
   Rom. I am some-what eas'd in this yet.
   Char (Onely friend)
To what vaine purpose do I make my sorrow,
Wayte on the triumph of their cruelty?
Or teach their pride from my humilitie,
To thinke it has orecome? They are determin'd
What they will do: and it may well become me,
To robbe them of the glory they expect
From my submisse intreaties.
   Rom. Thinke not so, Sir,
The difficulties that you incounter with,
Will crowne, the vndertaking ——— Heauen! you weepe:
And I could do so too, but that I know,
Theres more expected from the sonne and friend
Of him, whose fatall losse now shakes our natures,
Then sighs, or teares, (in which a village nurse
Or cunning strumpet, when her knaue is hangd,
May ouercome vs.) We are men (young Lord)
Let vs not do like women. To the Court,
And there speake like your birth: wake sleeping iustice,
Or dare the Axe. This is a way will sort
With what you are. I call you not to that
I will shrinke from my selfe, I will deserue
Your thankes, or suffer with you—O how brauely
That sudden fire of anger shewes in you!

                                 Giue

The Fatall Dowry.

Giue fuell to it, since you are on a shelfe,
Of extreme danger suffer like your selfe.   *Exeunt.*

*Enter Rochfort, Nouall Se. Charmi, Du Croye, Aduocates,
Beaumont, and Officers, and 3. Presidents.*

Du Croye. Your Lordship's seated, May this meeting proue
prosperous to vs, and to the generall good of *Burgundy*.
  Nou. Se. Speake to the poynt.
  Du Croy. Which is,
With honour to dispose the place and power
Of primier President, which this reuerent man
Graue *Rochfort*, (whom for honours sake I name)
Is purpos'd to resigne a place, my Lords,
In which he hath with such integrity,
Perform'd the first and best parts of a Iudge,
That as his life transcends all faire examples
Of such as were before him in *Dijon*,
So it remaines to those that shall succeed him,
A President they may imitate, but not equall.
  Roch. I may not sit to heare this.
  Du Croy. Let the loue
And thankfulnes we are bound to pay to goodnesse,
In this o'recome your modestie.
  Roch. My thankes
For this great fauour shall preuent your trouble.
The honourable trust that was impos'd
Vpon my weakenesse, since you witnesse for me,
It was not ill discharg'd, I will not mention,
Nor now, it age had not depriu'd me of
The little strength I had to gouerne well,
The Prouince that I vndertooke, forsake it.
  Nou. That we could lend you of our yeeres.
  Du Croy. Or strength.
  Nou. Or as you are, perswade you to continue
The noble exercise of your knowing iudgement.
  Roch. That may not be, nor can your Lordships goodnes,

Since

The Fatall Dowry.

Since your imployments haue confer'd vpon me
Sufficient wealth, deny the vse of it,
And though old age, when one foot's in the graue,
In many, when all humors else are spent
Feeds no affection in them, but desire
To adde height to the mountaine of their riches:
In me it is not so, I rest content
With the honours, and estate I now possesse,
And that I may haue liberty to vse,
What Heauen still blessing my poore industry,
Hath made me Master of: I pray the Court
To ease me of my burthen, that I may
Employ the small remainder of my life,
In liuing well, and learning how to dye so.

Enter Romont, and Charalois.

Rom. See sir, our Aduocate.

Du Croy. The Court intreats,
Your Lordship will be pleas'd to name the man,
Which you would haue your successor, and in me,
All promise to confirme it.

Roch. I embrace it,
As an assurance of their fauour to me,
And name my Lord *Nouall.*

Du Croy. The Court allows it.

Roch. But there are suters waite heere, and their causes
May be of more necessity to be heard,
And therefore wish that mine may be defer'd,
And theirs haue hearing.

Du Croy. If your Lordship please
To take the place, we will proceed.

Charm. The cause
We come to offer to your Lordships censure,
Is in it selfe so noble, that it needs not
Or Rhetorique in me that plead, or fauour
From your graue Lordships, to determine of it,
Since to the prayse of your impartiall iustice
(Which guilty, nay condemn'd men, dare not scandall)

C

The Fatall Dowry.

It will erect a trophy of your mercy
VVith married to that Iustice.
  Nou. Se. Speake to the cause.
  Charm. I will, my Lord: to say, the late dead Marshall
The father of this young Lord heere, my Clyent,
Hath done his Country great and faithfull seruice,
Might taske me of impertinence to repeate,
What your graue Lordships cannot but remember,
He in his life, become indebted to
These thriftie men, I will not wrong their credits,
By giuing them the attributes they now merit,
And fayling by the fortune of the warres,
Of meanes to free himselfe, from his ingagements,
He was arrested, and for want of bayle
Imprisond at their suite, and not long after
VVith losse of liberty ended his life.
And though it be a *Maxime* in our Lawes,
All suites dye with the person, these mens malice
In death find matter for their hate to worke on,
Denying him the decent Rytes of buriall,
VVhich the sworne enemies of the Christian faith
Grant freely to their slaues: in ay it therefore please
Your Lordships, so to fashion your decree,
That what their crueltie doth forbid, your pittie
May giue allowance to.
  Nou. Se. How long haue you Sir practis'd in Court?
  Charmi. Some twenty yeeres, my Lord.
  Nou. Se. By your grosse ignorance it should appeare,
Not twentie dayes.
  Charmi. I hope I haue giuen no cause in this, my Lord
  Nou. Se. How dare you moue the Court,
To the dispensing with an Act confirmd
By Parliment, to the terror of all banquerouts?
Go home, and with more care peruse the Statutes,
Or the next motion sauoring of this boldnesse,
May force you to leape (against your will)
Ouer the place you plead at.

Charmi.

The Fatall Dowry.

Carmi. I foresaw this.

Rom. Why does your Lordship thinke, the mouing of
A cause more honest then this Court had euer
The honor to determine, can deserue
A checke like this?

Non. Se. Strange boldnes!

Rom. Tis fit freedome:
Or do you conclude, an aduocate cannot hold
His credit with the Iudge, vnlesse he study
His face more then the cause for which he pleades?

Charmi. Forbeare.

Rom. Or cannot you, that haue the power
To qualifie the rigour of the Lawes
When you are pleased, take a little from
The strictnesse of your sowre decrees, enacted
In fauor of the greedy creditors
Against the orethrowne debter?

Non. Se. Sirra, you that prate
Thus sawcily, what are you?

Rom. Why Ile tell you,
Thou purple-colour'd man, I am one to whom
Thou owest the meanes thou hast of sitting there,
A corrupt Elder.

Charmi. Forbeare.

Rom. The nose thou wear'st, is my gift, and those eyes,
That meete no object so base as their Master,
Had bin, long since, torne from that guiltie head,
And thou thy selfe slaue to some needy Swisse,
Had I not worne a sword, and vs'd it better
Then in thy prayers thou ere didst thy tongue.

Non. Se. Shall such an Insolence passe vnpunisht?

Charmi. Heare mee.

Rom. Yet I, that in my seruice done my Country,
Disdaine to bee put in the scale with thee,
Confesse my selfe vnworthy to bee valued
VVith the least part, nay haire of the dead Marshall,
Of whose so many glorious vndertakings,

The Fatall Dowry.

Make choice of any one, and that the meanest
Performd against the subtill Fox of France,
The politique *Lewis*, or the more desperate Swisse,
And 'twyll outwaygh all the good purpose,
Though put in act, that euer Gowneman practizd.

   Non.Se. Away with him to prison.
   Rom. If that curses,
Vrg'd iustly, and breath'd forth so, euer fell
On those that did deserue them; let not mine
Be spent in vaine now, that thou from this instant
Mayest in thy feare that they will fall vpon thee,
Be sensible of the plagues they shall bring with them.
And for denying of a little earth,
To couer what remaynes of our great soldyer:
May all your wiues proue whores, your factors theenes,
And while you liue, your ryotous heires vndoe you.
And thou, the patron of their cruelty,
Of all thy Lordships liue not to be owner
Of so much dung as will conceale a Dog,
Or what is worse, thy selfe in. And thy yeeres,
To th'end thou mayst be wretched, I wish many,
And as thou hast denied the dead a graue,
May misery in thy life make thee desire one,
Which men and all the Elements keepe from thee:
I haue begun well, imitate, exceed.

   Roch. Good counsayle were it, a prayse worthy deed. *Ex.*
   Du. Croye. Remember what we are. *Officers with Rom.*
   Chara. Thus low my duty
Answeres your Lordships counsaile. I will vse
In the few words (with which I am to trouble
Your Lordships eares) the temper that you wish me:
Not that I feare to speake my thoughts as lowd,
And with a liberty beyond *Romont*:
But that I know, for me that am made vp
Of all that's wretched, so to haste my end,
Would seeme to most, rather a willingnesse
To quit the burthen of a hopelesse life,

                              Then

The Fatall Dowry.

Then scorne of death, or duty to the dead.
I therefore bring the tribute of my prayse
To your seueritie, and commend the Iustice,
That will not for the many seruices
That any man hath done the Common wealth,
Winke at his least of ills: what though my father
Writ man before he was so, and confirm'd it,
By numbring that day, no part of his life,
In which he did not seruice to his Country;
Was he to be free therefore from the Lawes,
And ceremonious forme in your decrees?
Or else because he did as much as man
In those three memorable ouerthrowes
At *Granson, Morat, Nancy*, where his Master,
The warlike *Charloyes* (with whose misfortunes
I beare his name) lost treasure, men and life,
To be excus'd, from payment of those summes
Which (his owne patri mony spent) his zeale,
To serue his Countrey, forc'd him to take vp?

   Nou. Se. The president were ill.
   Chara. And yet, my Lord, this much
I know youll grant; After those great defeatures,
Which in their dreadfull ruines buried quick, *Enter officers.*
Courage and hope, in all men but himselfe,
He forst the proud foe, in his height of conquest,
To yeeld vnto an honourable peace.
And in it saued an hundred thousand liues,
To end his owne, that was sure proofe against
The scalding Summers heate, and Winters frost,
Ill ayres, the Cannon, and the enemies sword,
In a most loathsome prison.
   Du Croy. Twas his fault to be so prodigall.
   Nou. Se. He had fr6 the state sufficient entertainment for
   Char. Sufficent? My Lord, you sit at home, (the Army.
And though your fees are boundlesse at the barre:
Are thriftie in the charges of the warre,
But your wills be obeyd. To these I turne,

C 3

The Fatall Dowry.

To these soft-hearted men, that wisely know
They are onely good men, that pay what they owe.
  2 *Cred.* And so they are.
  1 *Cred.* 'Tis the City Doctrine,
We stand bound to maintaine it.
    Char. Be constant in it,
And since you are as mercilesse in your natures,
As base, and mercenary in your meanes
By which you get your wealth, I will not vrge
The Court to take away one scruple from
The right of their lawes, or one good thought
In you to mend your disposition with.
I know there is no musique to your eares
So pleasing as the groanes of men in prison,
And that the teares of widows, and the cries
Of famish'd Orphants, are the feasts that take you.
That to be in your danger, with more care
Should be auoyded, then infectious ayre,
The loath'd embraces of diseased women,
A flatterers poyson, or the losse of honour.
Yet rather then my fathers reuerent dust
Shall want a place in that faire monument,
In which our noble Ancestors lye intomb'd,
Before the Court I offer vp my selfe
A prisoner for it: loade me with those yrons
That haue worne out his life, in my best strength
Ile run to th'incounter of cold hunger,
And choose my dwelling where no Sun dares enter,
So he may be releas'd.
  1 *Cred.* What meane you sir?
  2 *Aduo.* Onely your fee againe ther's so much sayd
Already in this cause, and sayd so well,
That should I onely offer to speake in it,
I should not bee heard, or laught at for it.
  1 *Cred.* 'Tis the first mony aduocate ere gaue backe,
Though hee sayd nothing.
Roch. Be aduis'd, young Lord,

                                 And

The Fatall Dowry.

And well confiderate, you throw away
Your liberty, and ioyes of life together:
Your bounty is imployd vpon a fubiect
That is not fenfible of it, with which, wife man
Neuer abus'd his goodneffe; the great vertues
Of your dead father vindicate themfelues,
From thefe mens malice, and breake ope the prifon,
Though it containe his body.

Nou. Se. Let him alone,
If he loue Lords, a Gods name let him weare 'em,
Prouided thefe confent.

Char. I hope they are not
So ignorant in any way of profit,
As to neglect a poffibility
To get their owne, by feeking it from that
Which can returne them nothing, but ill fame,
And curfes for their barbarous cruelties.

3 *Cred.* What thinke you of the offer?
2 *Cred.* Very well.
1 *Cred.* Accept it by all meanes: let's fhut him vp,
He is well-fhaped and has a villanous tongue,
And fhould he ftudy that way of renenge,
As I dare almoft fweare he loues a wench,
We haue no wiues, nor neuer fhall get daughters
That will hold out againft him.

Du Croy. What's your anfwer?
2 *Cred.* Speake you for all.
1 *Cred.* Why, let our executions
That lye vpon the father, bee return'd
Vpon the fonne, and we releafe the body.

Nou. Se. The Court muft grant you that.
Char. I thanke your Lordfhips,
They haue in it confirm'd on me fuch glory,
As no time can take from me: I am ready,
Come lead me where you pleafe: captiuity
That comes with honour, is true liberty.

Exit Charmi, Cred. & Officers.

The Fatall Dowry.

Nou. Se. Strange rashnesse.

Roch. A braue resolution rather,
Worthy a better fortune, but howeuer
It is not now to be disputed, therefore
To my owne cause. Already I haue found
Your Lordships bountifull in your fauours to me;
And that should teach my modesty to end heere
And presse your loues no further.

Du Croy. There is nothing
The Court can grant, but with assurance you
May aske it, and obtaine it.

Roch. You incourage a bold Petitioner, and 'tis not fit
Your fauours should be lost. Besides, 'cas beene
A custome many yeeres, at the surrendring
The place I now giue vp, to grant the President
One boone, that parted with it. And to confirme
Your grace towards me, against all such as may
Detract my actions, and life hereafter,
I now preferre it to you.

Du Croy. Speake it freely.

Roch. I then desire the liberty of *Romont*,
And that my Lord *Nouall*, whose priuate wrong
Was equall to the iniurie that was done
To the dignity of the Court, will pardon it,
And now signe his enlargement.

Nou. Se. Pray you demand
The moyety of my estate, or any thing
Within my power, but this.

Roch. Am I denyed then—my first and last request?

Du Croy. It must not be.

2. *Pre.* I haue a voyce to giue in it.

3. *Pre.* And I.
And if perswasion will not worke him to it,
We will make knowne our power.

Nou. Se. You are too violent,
You shall haue my consent.——But would you had
Made tryall of my loue in any thing

But

The Fatall Dowry

But this, you should haue found then——But it skills not,
You haue what you desire.

Roch. I thanke your Lordships.

Du Croy. The court is vp, make way. *Ex. omnes, præter*
Roch. I follow you——*Baumont.* *Roch. & Baumont.*

Baum. My Lord.

Roch. You are a scholler, *Baumont*,
And can search deeper into th' intents of men,
Then those that are lesse knowing——How appear'd
The piety and braue behauiour of
Young *Charloyes* to you?

Baum. It is my wonder,
Since I want language to expresse it fully;
And sure the Collonell——

Roch. Fie! he was faulty——what present mony haue I?

Baum. There is no want
Of any summe a priuate man has vse for.

Roch. 'Tis well,
I am strangely taken with this *Charaloyes*;
Methinkes, from his example, the whole age
Should learne to be good, and continue so.
Vertue workes strangely with vs, and his goodnesse
Rising aboue his fortune, seemes to me
Princelike, to will, not aske a courtesie. *Exeunt.*

Act. secundus. Scæna prima:

Enter Pontalier, Malotin, Baumont.

Mal. Tis strange.

Baum. Me thinkes so,

Pont. In a man, but young,
Yet old in iudgement, theorique, and practicke,
In all humanity (and to increase the wonder)
Religious,

The Fatall Dowry

Religious, yet a Souldier, that he should
Yeeld his free liuing youth a captiue, for
The freedome of his aged fathers Corpes,
And rather choose to want lifes necessaries,
Liberty, hope of fortune, then it should
In death be kept from Christian ceremony.

 Malo. Come, 'Tis a golden president in a Sonne,
To let strong nature haue the better hand,
(In such a case) of all affected reason.
What yeeres sits on this *Charolois*?

 Baum. Twenty eight, for since the clocke did strike him
Vnder his fathers wing, this Sonne hath fought,
Seru'd and commanded, and so aptly both,
That sometimes he appear'd his fathers father,
And neuer lesse then's sonne; the old mans vertues
So recent in him, as the world may sweare,
Nought but a faire tree, could such fayre fruit beare.

 Pont. But wherefore lets he such a barbarous law,
And men more barbarous to execute it,
Preuaile on his soft disposition,
That he had rather dye aliue for debt
Of the old man in prison, then he should
Rob him of Sepulture, considering
These monies borrow'd bought the lenders peace,
And all their meanes they inioy, nor was diffus'd
In any impious or licencious path?

 Bau. True: for my part, were it my fathers trunke,
The tyrannous Ram-heads, with their hornes should gore it,
Or, cast it to their curres (than they) lesse currish,
Ere prey on me so, with their Lion-law,
Being in my free will (as in his) to shun it.

 Pont. Alasse! he knowes himselfe (in pouerty) lost:
For in this parciall auaricious age
What price beares Honor? Vertue? Long agoe
It was but prays'd, and freez'd, but now a dayes
'Tis colder far, and has, nor loue, nor praise,
Very prayse now freezeth too: for nature

            Did

The Fatall Dowry.

Did make the heathen, far more Christian then,
Then knowledge vs (lesse heathenish) Christian.
 Malo. This morning is the funerall.
 Pont. Certainely!
And from this prison 'twas the sonnes request
That his deare father might incerment haue. *Recorders*
See, the young sonne interd a liuely graue. *Musique.*
 Baum. They come, obserue their order.

Enter Funerall, Body borne by 4. Captaines and Souldiers, Mourners, Scutchions, and very good order. Charolois, and Romont meet it. Char. speaks. Rom. weeping, solemne Musique, 3 Creditors.

 Char. How like a silent streame shaded with night,
And gliding softly with our windy sighes;
Moues the whole frame of this solemnity!
Teares, sighes and blackes, filling the fimily,
Whilst I the onely murmur in this groue
Of death, thus hollowly break forth! Vouchsafe
To stay a while, rest, rest in peace, deare earth,
Thou that brought'st rest to their vnthankfull lyues,
Whose cruelty deny'd thee rest in death:
Heere stands thy poore Executor thy sonne,
That makes his life prisoner, to bale thy death;
Who gladlier puts on this captiuity,
Then Virgins long in loue, their wedding weeds:
Of all that euer thou hast done good to,
These onely haue good memories, for they
Remember best, forget not gratitude.
I thanke you for this last and friendly loue.
And tho this Country, like a viperous mother,
Not onely hath eate vp vngratefully
All meanes of thee her sonne, but last thy selfe,
Leauing thy heire so bare and indigent,
He cannot rayse thee a poore Monument,
Such as a flatterer, or a vsurer hath.

D 2 Thy

The Fatall Dowry.

Thy worth, in euery honest brest buyldes one,
Making their friendly hearts thy funerall stone.
  Pont. Sir.
  Char. Peace, O peace, this sceane is wholy mine.
What weepe ye, souldiers? Blanch not, *Romont* weepes.
Ha, let me see, my miracle is cas'd,
The iaylors and the creditors do weepe;
Euen they that make vs weepe, do weepe themselues.
Be these thy bodies balme : these and thy vertue
Keepe thy fame euer odoriferous,
Whilst the great, proud, rich, vndeseruing man,
Aliue stinkes in his vices, and being vanish'd,
The golden calfe that was an Idoll deckt
With Marble pillars Iet, and Porphyrie,
Shall quickly both in bone and name consume,
Though wrapt in lead, spice, Searecloth and perfume
  1 *Cred.* Sir.
  Char. What! Away for shame : you prophane rogues
Must not be mingled with these holy reliques :
This is a Sacrifice, our showre shall crowne
His sepulcher with Oliue, Myrrh and Bayes
The plants of peace, of sorrow, victorie,
Your teares would spring but weedes.
  1 *Cred.* Would they not so ?
Wee'll keepe them to stop bottles then :
  Rom. No; keepe 'em for your owne sins, you Rogues,
Till you repent : you'll dye else and be damn'd.
  2 *Cred.* Damn'd, ha! ha, ha.
  Rom. Laugh yee?
  3 *Cred.* Yes faith. Sir, weel'd be very glad
To please you eyther way.
  1 *Cred.* Y'are ne're content,
Crying nor laughing.
  Rom. Both with a birth shee rogues.
  2 *Cred.* Our wiues, Sir, taught vs.
  Rom. Looke, looke you slaues, your thanklesse cruelty
And sauage manners, of vnkind *Dijon*,

Exhaust

The Fatall Dowry.

Exhauft thefe flouds, and not his fathers death.
   1 Cred. Slid, Sir, what would yee, ye'are fo cholericke?
   2 Cred. Moft fouldiers are fo yfaith, let him alone:
They haue little elfe to liue on, we haue not had
A penny of him, haue wee?
   3 Cred. Slight, wo'd you haue our hearts?
   1 Cred. We haue nothing but his body heere in durance
For all our mony.
   Prieft. On.
   Char. One moment more,
But to beftow a few poore legacyes,
All I haue left in my dead fathers rights,
And I haue done. Captaine, weare thou thefe fpurs
That yet ne're made his horfe runne from a foe.
Lieutenant, thou; this Scarfe, and may it tye
Thy valor, and thy honeftie together:
For fo it did in him. Enfigne, this Curace
Your Generalls necklace once. You gentle Bearers,
Deuide this purfe of gold; this other, ftrow
Among the poore: tis all I haue. *Romont,*
(Weare thou this medall of himfelfe) that like
A hearty Oake, grew'ft clofe to this tall Pine,
Euen in the wildeft wildernefse of war,
VVhereon foes broke their fwords, and tyr'd themfelues;
VVounded and hack'd yee were, but neuer fell'd.
For me, my portion prouide in Heauen:
My roote is earth'd, and I a defolate branch
Left fcattered in the high way of the world,
Trod vnder foot, that might haue bin a Columne,
Mainely fupporting our demolifh'd houfe;
This would I weare as my inheritance.
And what hope can arife to me from it,
VVhen I and it are both heere prifoners?
Onely may this, if euer we be free,
Keepe, or redeeme me from all infamie.   *Song. Muficke.*
   1 Cred. No farther, looke to'em at your owne perill.
   2 Cred. No, as they pleafe: their Mafter's a good man.

D 3

The Fatall Dowry.

I would they were the *Burmudas*.

Saylor. You must no further.
The prisonlimits you, and the Creditors
Exact the strictnesse.

Rom. Out you wooluish mungrells!
Whose braynes should be knockt out, like dogs in Iuly,
Lest your infection poyson a whole towne.

Char. They grudge our sorrow: your ill wills perforce
Turnes now to Charity: they would not haue vs
Walke too farre mourning, vsurers reliefe
Grieues, if the Debtors haue too much of griefe. *Exeunt.*

Enter Beaumelle : Florimell : Bellapert.

Beau. I prithee tell me, *Florimell*, why do women marry?

Flor. Why truly Madam, I thinke, to lye with their husbands.

Bella. You are a foole; She lyes, Madam, women marry
To lye with other men. (husbands.

Flor. Faith, eene such a woman wilt thou make. By this
light, Madam, this wagtaile will spoyle you, if you take
delight in her licence.

Beau. Tis true, *Florimell*: and thou wilt make me too good
for a yong Lady. What an electuary found my father out for
his daughter, when hee compounded you two my women?
for thou, *Florimell*, art eene a graine too heauy, simply for a
wayting Gentlewoman.

Flor. And thou *Bellapert*, a graine too light.

Bella. Well, go thy wayes goodly wisdom, whom no body
regards. I wonder, whether be elder thou or thy hood: you
thinke, because you serue my Ladyes mother, are 32 yeeres
old which is a peepe out, you know.

Flor. Well sayd, wherligig.

Bella. You are deceyu'd: I want a peg ith' middle.
Out of these Prerogatiues! you thinke to be mother of the
maydes heere, & mortifie em with prouerbs: goe, goe, gouern
the sweet meates, and waigh the Suger, that the wenches
steale none: say your prayers twice a day, and as I take it, you
haue

The Fatall Dowry:

haue perform'd your function.

Flor. I may bee euen with you.

Bell. Harke, the Court's broke vp. Goe helpe my old Lord out of his Caroch, and scratch his head till dinner time.

Flor. Well.   *Exit.*

Bell. Fy Madam, how you walke! By my mayden-head you looke 7 yeeres older then you did this morning: why, there can be nothing vnder the Sunne valuable, to make you thus a minute.

Beau. Ah my sweete *Bellapert* thou Cabinet
To all my counsels, thou'dost know the cause
That makes thy Lady wither thus in youth.

Bel. Vd'd-light, enioy your wishes: whilst I liue,
One way or other you shall crowne your will.
Would you haue him your husband that you loue,
And, can't not bee? he is your seruant though,
And may performe the office of a husband.

Beau. But there is honor, wench.

Bell. Such a disease
There is in deed, for which ere I would dy.

Beau. Prethee, distinguish me a mayd & wife.

Bell. Faith, Madam, one may beare any mans children, Tother must beare no mans.

Beau. What is a husband?

Bell. Physicke, that tumbling in your belly, will make you sicke ith' stomacke: the onely distinction betwixt a husband and a seruant is: the first will lye with you, when hee please; the last shall lye with you when you please. Pray tell me, Lady, do you loue, to marry after, or would you marry, to loue after?

Beau. I would meete loue and marriage both at once.

Bell. Why then you are out of the fashion, and wilbe contemn'd: for (Ile assure you) there are few women i'ch world, but either they haue married first, and loue after, or loue first, and marryed after: you must do as you may, not as you would: your fathers will is the Goale you must fly to: if a husband approch you, you would haue further off, is he your
loue,

The Fatall Dowry.

loue? the lesse neere you. A husband in these dayes is but a cloake to bee oftner layde vpon your bed, then in your bed.

Baum. Humpe.

Bell. Sometimes you may weare him on your shoulder, now and then vnder your arme: but seldome or neuer let him couer you: for 'tis not the fashion.

Enter y. Nouall, Pontalier, Malotin, Liladam, Aymer.

Nou. Best day to natures curiosity,
Starre of *Dijum*, the lustre of all *France*,
Perpetuall spring dwell on thy rosy cheekes,
Whose breath is perfume to our Continent,
See *Flora* turn'd in her varieties.

Bell. Oh diuine Lord!

Nou. No autumne, nor no age euer approach
This heauenly piece, which nature hauing wrought,
She lost her needle and did then despaire,
Euer to worke so liuely and so faire.

Lilad. Vds light, my Lord, one of the purles of your band is (without all discipline falne) out of his ranke.

Nou. How? I would not for a 1000 crownes she had seen't. Deare *Liladam*, reforme it.

Bell. Oh Lord: *Per se*, Lord, quintessence of honour, shee walkes not vnder a weede that could deny thee any thing.

Baum. Prethy peace, wench, thou dost but blow the fire, that flames too much already. *Lilad. Aym. trim Nouall,*

Aym. By gad, my Lord, you haue the diui- *whilst Bell her* nest Taylor of Christendome; he hath made *Lady.* you looke like an Angell in your cloth of Tissue doublet.

Pont. This is a three-leg'd Lord, ther's a fresh assault, oh that men should spend time thus!
See see, how her blood driues to her heart, and straight vaults to her cheekes againe.

Malo. What are these?

Pont. One of 'em there the lower is a good, foolish, knauish, sociable gallimaufry of a man, and has much taught

my

The Fatall Dowry.

my Lord with singing, hee is master of a musicke house: the other is his dressing blocke, vpon whom my Lord layes all his cloathes, and fashions, ere he vouchsafes 'em his owne person; you shall see him i'th morning in the Gally-foyst, at noone in the Bullion, i'th euening in Quirpo, and all night in ———

Malo. A Bawdyhouse.

Pont. If my Lord deny, they deny, if hee affirme, they affirme: they skip into my Lords cast skins some twice a yeere, and thus they liue to eate, eate to liue, and liue to prayse my Lord.

Malo. Good sir, tell me one thing.

Pont. What's that?

Malo. Dare these men euer fight, on any cause?

Pont. Oh no, 'twould spoyle their cloathes, and put their bands out of order.

Non. Mrs, you heare the news: your father has resign'd his Presidentship to my Lord my father.

Malo. And Lord *Charolois* vndone foreuer.

Pont. Troth, 'tis pity, sir.
A brauer hope of so assur'd a father
Did neuer comfort *France*.

Lila. A good dumbe mourner.

Aym. A silent blacke.

Non. Oh fie vpon him, how he weares his cloathes!
As if he had come this Christmas from St. *Omers*,
To see his friends, and return'd after Twelfetyde.

Lilad. His Colonell lookes fienely like a drouer,

Non. That had a winter ly'n perdieu i'th rayne.

Aym. What, he that weares a clout about his necke,
His cuffes in's pocket, and his heart in's mouth?

Non. Now out vpon him!

Beau. Seruant, tye my hand.
How your lips blush, in scorne that they should pay
Tribute to hands, when lips are in the way!

Non. I thus recant, yet now your hand looks white,
Because your lips robd it of such a right.

B

Mounsteur

The Fatall Dowry.

Monsieur Aymont, I prethy sing the song
Deuoted to my Mris.   *Cant.*   *Musicke.*
  After the Song, Enter Rochfort, & Baumont.
 Baum. Romont will come, sir, straight.
 Roch. 'Tis well.
 Beau. My Father.
 Nouall. My honorable Lord.
 Roch. My Lord *Nouall*, this is a vertue in you,
So early vp and ready before noone,
That are the map of dressing through all *France*.
 Nou. I rise to say my prayers, sir, heere's my Saint.
 Roch. Tis well and courtly: you must giue me leaue,
I haue some priuate conference with my daughter,
Pray vse my garden, you shall dine with me.
 Lilad. Wee'l waite on you.
 Nou. Good morne vnto your Lordship,
Remember what you haue vow'd———to his Mris. *Exeunt*
 Beau. Performe I must. *omnes, prater Roch. Daug.*
 Roch. Why how now *Beaumelle*, thou look'st not well,
Th'art sad of late, come cheere thee, I haue found
A wholesome remedy for these mayden fits,
A goodly Oake whereon to twist my vine,
Till her faire branches grow vp to the starres.
Be neere at hand, successe crowne my intent,
My businesse fills my little time so full,
I cannot stand to talke: I know, thy duty
Is handmayd to my will, especially
When it presents nothing but good and fit.
 Beau. Sir, I am yours. Oh if my teares proue true, *Exit*
Fate hath wrong'd loue, and will destroy me too. *Daug*
   Enter Romonts keeper.
 Rom. Sent you for me, sir?
 Roch. Yes.
 Rom. Your Lordships pleasure?
 Roch. Keeper, this prisoner I will see forthcomming
Vpon my word--- Sit downe good Colonell. *Exit keeper.*
Why I did wish you hither, noble sir,

The Fatall Dowry.

Is to aduise you from this yron carriage,
Which, so affected, *Romont*, you weare,
To pity and to counsell yee submit
With expedition to the great *Novall*:
Recant your sterne contempt, and slight neglect
Of the whole Court, and him, and opportunity,
Or you will vndergoe a heauy censure
In publique very shortly.

  Rom. Hum hum: reuerend sir,
I haue obseru'd you, and doe know you well,
And am now more affraid you know not me,
By wishing my submission to *Novall*,
Then I can be of all the bellowing mouthes
That waite vpon him to pronounce the censure,
Could it determine me torments, and shame.
Submit, and craue forgiuenesse of a beast!
Tis true, this bile of state weares purple Tissue,
Is high fed, proud, so is his Lordships horse,
And beares as rich Caparisons. I know,
This Elephant carries on his backe not onely
Towres, Castles, but the ponderous republique,
And neuer stoops for't, with his strong breath trunk
Snuffes others titles, Lordships, Offices,
Wealth, bribes and lyues, vnder his rauenous iawes,
Whats this vnto my freedome? I dare dye;
And therfore aske this Cammell, if these blessings
(For so they would be vnderstood by a man)
But mollifie one rudenesse in his nature,
Sweeten the eager relish of the law,
At whose great helme he sits: helps he the poore
In a iust businesse? nay, does he not crosse
Euery deserued souldier and scholler,
As if when nature made him, she had made
The generall Antipathy of all vertue?
How sauagely, and blasphemously hee spake
Touching the Generall, the graue Generall dead,
I must weepe when I thinke on't.

Roch. Sir.   E 2   *Rom.*

The Fatall Dowry.

Rom. My Lord, I am not stubborne, I can melt, you see,
And prize a vertue better then my life:
For though I be not learnd, I euer lou'd
That ho'y Mother of all issues, good,
VVhose white hand (for a Scepter) holdes a File
To pollish roughest customes, and in you
She has her right: see, I am calme as sleepe,
But when I thinke of the grosse iniuries,
The godlesse wrong done, to my Generall dead,
I raue indeed, and could eate this *Nouall*
A soule-lesse Dromodary.

Roch. Oh bee temperate,
Sir, though I would perswade, I'le not constraine:
Each mans opinion freely is his owne,
Concerning any thing or any body,
Be it right or wrong, tis at the Iudges perill.

Enter Baumond.

Bau. These men, Sir, waite without, my Lord is come too.

Roch. Pay 'em those summes vpon the table, take
Their full releases: stay, I want a witnesse:
Let mee intreat you Colonell, to walke in,
And stand but by, to see this money pay'd,
It does concerne you and your friends, it was
The better cause you were sent for, though sayd otherwise.
The deed shall make this my request more plaine.

Rom. I shall obey your pleasure Sir, though ignorant
To what is tends?   *Exit Seruant: Roment.*

Roch. Worthiest Sir,   *Enter Charolois.*
You are most welcome: fye, no more of this:
You haue out-wept a woman, noble *Charolois.*
No man but has, or must bury a father.

Char. Graue Sir, I buried sorrow, for his death,
In the graue with him. I did neuer thinke
Hee was immortall, though I vow I grieue,
And see no reason why the vicious,
Vertuous, valiant and vnworthy men
Should dye alike.

Roch.

The Fatall Dowry.

Roch. They do not.

Char. In the manner
Of dying, Sir, they do not, but all dye,
And therein differ not: but I haue done.
I spy'd the lively picture of my father,
Passing your gallery, and that cast this water
Into mine eyes: see, foolish that I am,
To let it doe so.

Roch. Sweete and gentle nature,
How silken is this well comparatiuely
To other men! I haue a suite to you Sir.

Char. Take it, tis granted.   *Roch.* VVhat?

Char. Nothing, my Lord.

Roch. Nothing is quickly granted.

Chara. Faith, my Lord,
That nothing granted, is euen all I haue,
For (all know) I haue nothing left to grant.

Roch. Sir, ha' you any suite to me? Ill grant
You something, any thing.

Char. Nay surely, I that can
Giue nothing, will but sue for that againe.
No man will grant mee any thing I sue for,
But begging nothing, euery man will giue't.

Roch. Sir, the loue I bore your father, and the worth
I see in you, so much resembling his,
Made me thus send for you. And tender heere   *Drawes a*
What euer you will take, gold, Ieweis, both,   *Curtayne.*
All, to supply your wants, and free your selfe.
Where heauenly vertue in high blouded veines
Is lodg'd, and can agree, men should kneele downe,
Adore, and sacrifice all that they haue;
And well they may, it is so seldome seene.
Put off your wonder, and heere freely take
Or send your seruants. Nor, Sir, shall you vse
In ought of this, a poore mans fee, or bribe,
Vniustly taken of the rich, but what's
Directly gotten, and yet by the Law.

E 3   *Char.*

The Fatall Dowry.

Char. How ill, Sir, it becomes those haires to mocke?
Roch. Mocke? thunder strike mee then.
Char. You doe amaze mee:
But you shall wonder too, I will not take
One single piece of this great heape: why should I
Borrow, that haue not meanes to pay, nay am
A very bankerupt, euen in flattering hope
Of euer raysing any. All my begging,
Is *Romonts* libertie. *Enter Romont, Creditors loaden with mony. Baumont.*
Roch. Heere is your friend,
Enfranchisd ere you spake. I giue him you,
And *Charolois.* I giue you to your friend
As free a man as hee; your fathers debts
Are taken off.
Char. How?
Rom. Sir, it is most true.
I am the witnes.
1 *Cred.* Yes faith, wee are pay'd.
2 *Cred.* Heauen blesse his Lordship, I did thinke him wiser.
3 *Cred.* He a states-man, he an asse Pay other mens debts?
4 *Cred.* That hee was neuer bound for.
Rom. One more such would saue the rest of pleaders.
Char. Honord *Rochfort.*
Lye still my toung and bushes, cal'd my cheekes,
That offer thankes in words, for such great deeds.
Roch. Call in my daughter: still I haue a suit to you. *Baum.*
VVould you requite mee. *Exit.*
Rom. VVith his life, assure you.
Roch. Nay, would you make me now your debter, Sir?
This is my onely child: what shee appeares, *Enter Baum.*
Your Lordship well may see her education, *Beau.*
Followes not any; for her mind, I know it
To be far fayrer then her shape, and hope
It will continue so: if now her birth
Be not too meane for *Charolois*, take her
This virgin by the hand, and call her wife,
Indowd with all my fortunes: blesse mee so.

Requite

The Fatall Dowry.

Requite mee thus, and make mee happier,
In ioyning my poore empty name to yours,
Then if my state were multiplied ten fold.
   Char. Is this the payment, Sir, that you expect?
Why, you participate me more in debt,
That nothing but my life can euer pay,
This beautie being your daughter, in which yours
I must conceiue necessitie of her vertue
Without all dowry is a Princes ayme,
Then, as shee is, for poore and worthlesse I,
How much too worthy! Waken me, *Romont*,
That I may know I dream't, and find this vanisht
  Rom. Sure, I sleepe not.
  Roch. Your sentence life or death.
  Char. Faire *Beaumelle*, can you loue me?
  Beau. Yes, my Lord.   *Enter Nowall, Ponta,*
  Char. You need not question me, if I can you. *Malotine,*
You are the fayrest virgin in *Digam.*   *Lilad, Aymer. All*
And *Rochfort* is your father.   *salute.*
  Nou. What's this change?
  Roch. You met my wishes, Gentlemen.
  Rom. VVhat make
These dogs in doublets he ere?
  Beau. A Visitation, Sir.
  Char. Then thus, Faire *Beaumelle*, I write my faith
Thus seale it in the sight of Heauen and men.
Your fingers tye my heart-strings with this touch
In true-loue knots, which nought but death shall loose,
And yet these eares (an Embleme of our loues)
Like Cristall riuers indiuidually
Flow into one another, make one soarce,
Which neuer man distinguish, lesse deuide:
Breath, marry, breath, and kisses, mingle soules,
Two hearts, and bodies, heere incorporate:
And though with little wooing I haue wonne,
My future life shall bee a wooing tyme.
And euery day, new as the bridall one,

The Fatall Dowry.

Oh Sir, I groane vnder your courtesies,
More then my fathers bones vnder his wrongs,
You *Curtius*-like, haue throwne into the gulfe,
Of this his Countries foule ingratitude,
Your life and fortunes, to redeeme their shames.

Roch. No more, my glory, come, let's in and hasten
This celebration.   *Rom. Mal. Pont. Bau.*
All faire blisse vpon it.
                                    Exeunt Roch. Char. Rom. Bau. Mal.

Nou. Mistresse.
Beau. Oh seruant, vertue strengthen me.
Thy presence blowes round my affections vane:
You will vndoe me, if you speake againe.   *Exit Beaum.*
Lilad. Aym. Here will be sport for you. This workes.
                                    Exeunt Lilad. Aym.

Nou. Peace, peace.
Pont. One word, my Lord *Nouall*.
Nou. What, thou wouldst mony; there.
Pont. No, Ile none, Ile not be bought a slaue,
A Pander, or a Parasite, for all
Your fathers worth, though you haue sau'd my life,
Rescued me often from my wants, I must not
Winke at your follyes: that will ruine you.
You know my blunt way, and my loue to truth;
Forsake the pursuit of this Ladies honour,
Now you doe see her made another mans,
And such a mans, so good, so popular,
Or you will plucke a thousand mischiefes on you,
The benefits you haue done me, are not lost,
Nor cast away, they are purs'd heere in my heart,
But let me pay you, sir, a fayrer way
Then to defend your vices, or to sooth'em.

Nou. Ha, ha, ha, what are my courses vnto thee?
Good Cousin *Pontalier*, meddle with that
That shall concerne thy selfe.   *Exit Nouall.*
Pont. No more but scorne?

Moue

The Fatall Dowry.

Moue on then, starres, worke your pernicious will,
Onely the wise rule, and preuent your ill. *Exit.*
Hoboyes.

Here a passage ouer the Stage, while the Act is playing for the Marriage of Charalois with Beaumelle, &c.

Actus tertius, Scæna prima.

Enter Nouall Iunior, Bellapert.

Nou.In. Flie not to these excuses: thou hast bin
False in thy promise, and when I haue said
Vngratefull, all is spoke.

Bell. Good my Lord, but heare me onely.

Nou. To what purpose, trifler?
Can any thing that thou canst say, make voyd
The marriage? or those pleasures but a dreame,
Which *Charaloyes* (oh *Venus*) hath enioyd?

Bell. I yet could say that you receiue aduantage,
In what you thinke a losse, would you vouchsafe me
That you were neuer in the way till now
With safety to arriue at your desires,
That pleasure makes loue to you vnattended
By danger or repentance?

Nou. That I could.
But apprehend one reason how this might be,
Hope would not then forsake me.

Bell. The enioying
Of what you most desire, I say th' enioying
Shall, in the full possession of your wishes,
Confirme that I am faithfull.

Nou. Giue some rellish
How this may appeare possible.

Bell. I will

F Rel

The Fatall Dowry.

Rellish, and taste, and make the banquet easie:
You say my Ladie's married. I confesse it,
That *Charalois* hath inioyed her, 'tis most true
That with her, hee's already Master of
The best part of my old Lords state. Still better,
But that the first, or last, should be your hindrance,
I vtterly deny: for but obserue me:
While she went for, and was, I sweare, a Virgin,
What courtesie could she with her honour giue
Or you receiue with safety—take me with you;
When I say courtesie, doe not thinke I meane
A kisse, the tying of her shoo or garter,
An houre of priuate conference: those are trifles.
In this word courtesy, we that are gamesters point at
The sport direct, where not alone the louer
Brings his Artillery, but vses it,
Which word expounded to you, such a courtesie
Doe you expect, and sudden.

  Nou. But he tasted the first sweetes, *Bellapert*.
  Bell. He wrong'd you shrewdly,
He toyl'd to climbe vp to the *Phœnix* nest,
And in his prints leaues your ascent more easie.
I doe not know, you that are perfect Crittiques
In womens bookes, may talke of maydenheads.
  Nou. But for her marriage.
  Bell. 'Tis a faire protection
'Gainst all arrests of feare, or shame for euer.
Such as are faire, and yet not foolish, study
To haue one at thirteene; but they are mad
That stay till twenty. Then sir, for the pleasure,
To say Adu'terie's sweeter, that is stale.
This onely is not the contentment more,
To say, This is my Cuckold, then my Riuall.
More I could say—but briefely, she dotes on you,
If it proue otherwise, spare not, poyson me
With next gold you giue me.   *Enter Beaumelj.*
  Beau. Hows this seruant, courting my woman?
  Bell. As an entrance to

                             The

The Fatall Dowry.

The fauour of the mistris: you are together
And I am perfect in my qu.
 Beau. Stay *Bellapert.*
 Bell. In this, I must not with your leaue obey you.
Your Taylor and your Tire-woman waite without
And stay my counsayle, and direction for
Your next dayes dressing. I haue much to doe,
Nor will your Ladiship know, time is precious,
Continue idle: this choice Lord will finde
So fit imployment for you.   *Exit Bellap.*
 Beau. I shall grow angry.
 Nou. Not so, you haue a iewell in her, Madame
 Bell. I had forgot to tell your Ladiship   *Enter*
The closet is priuate and your couch ready;   *againe.*
And if you please that I shall loose the key,
But say so, and tis done.   *Exit Bellap.*
 Baum. You come to chide me, seruant, and bring with you
Sufficient warrant, you will say and truely,
My father found too much obedience in me,
By being won too soone: yet if you please
But to remember, all my hopes and fortunes
Had reuerence to this likening: you will grant
That though I did not well towards you, I yet
Did wisely for my selfe.
 Nou. With too much feruor
I haue so long lou'd and still loue you, Mistresse,
To esteeme that an iniury to me
Which was to you conuenient: that is past
My helpe, is past my cure. You yet may, Lady,
In recompence of all my dutious seruice,
(Prouided that your will answere your power)
Become my Creditresse.
 Beau. I vnderstand you,
And for assurance, the request you make
Shall not be long vnanswered. Pray you sit,
And by what you shall heare, you'l easily finde,
My passions are much fitter to desire,
    F 2   Then

The Fatall Dowry.

Then to be sued to.   *Enter Romont and Florimell.*

  Flor. Sir, tis not enuy
At the start my fellow has got of me in
My Ladies good opinion, thats the motiue
Of this discouery; but due payment
Of what I owe her Honour.
  Rom. So I conceiue it.
  Flo. I haue obseru'd too much, nor shall my silence
Preuent the remedy——yonder they are,
I dare not bee seene with you. You may doe
What you thinke fit, which wilbe, I presume,
The office of a faithfull and tryed friend
To my young Lord.   *Exit Flori.*
  Rom. This is no vision: ha!
  Nou. With the next opportunity.
  Beau. By this kisse, and this, and this.
  Nou. That you would euer sweare thus.
  Rom. If I seeme rude, your pardon, Lady; yours
I do not aske: come, do not dare to shew mee
A face of anger, or the least dislike,
Put on, and suddaily a milder looke,
I shall grow rough else.
  Nou. What haue I done, Sir,
To draw this harsh vnsauory language from you?
  Rom. Done, Popinjay? why, dost thou thinke that if
I ere had dreamt that thou hadst done me wrong,
Thou shouldest outliue it?
  Beau. This is something more
Then my Lords friendship giues commission for.
  Nou. Your presence and the place, makes him presume
Vpon my patience.
  Rom. As if thou ere wer't angry
But with thy Taylor, and yet that poore shred
Can bring more to the making vp of a man,
Then can be hop'd from thee: thou art his creature,
And did hee not each morning new create

                                              Thou

The Fatall Dowry.

Thou wouldst stinke and be forgotten. Ile not change
On sillable more with thee, vntill thou bring
Some testimony vnder good mens hands,
Thou art a Christian. I suspect thee strongly,
And wilbe satisfied: till which time, keepe from me.
The entertaiment of your visitation
Has made what I intended on a businesse.

Nou. So wee shall meete ——Madam.

Rom. Vse that legge againe, and Ile cut off the other.

Nou. Very good.   *Exit Nouall.*

Rom. What a perfume the Muske-cat leaues behind him!
Do you admit him for a property,
To saue you charges, Lady.

Beau. Tis not vselesse,
Now you are to succeed him.

Rom. So I respect you,
Not for your selfe, but in remembrance of,
Who is your father, and whose wife you now are,
That I choose rather not to vnderstand
Your nasty scoffe then, ————

Beau. What, you will not beate mee,
If I expound it to you. Heer's a Tyrant
Spares neyther man nor woman.

Rom. My intents
Madam, deserue not this; nor do I stay
To bee the whetstone of your wit: preserue it
To spend on such, as know how to admire
Such coloured stuffe. In me there is now speaks to you
As true a friend and seruant to your Honour,
And one that will with as much hazzard guard it,
As euer man did goodnesse.———— But then Lady,
You must endeauour not alone to bee,
But to appeare worthy such loue and seruice.

Beau. To what tends this?

Rom. Why, to this purpose, Lady,
I do desire you should proue such a wife
To *Charaloys* (and such a one hee merits)

F 3

The Fatall Dowry.

As Cæsar, did hee liue, could not except at,
Not onely innocent from crime, but free
From all taynt and suspition.
   Beau. They are base that iudge me otherwise.
   Rom. But yet bee carefull.
Detraction's a bold monster, and feares not
To wound the fame of Princes, if it find
But any blemish in their liues to worke on.
But ile bee plainer with you: had the people
Bin learnd to speake, but what euen now I saw,
Their malice out of that would raise an engine
To ouerthrow your honor. In my sight
(With yonder pointed foole I frighted from you)
You vs'd familiarity beyond
A modest entertaynment: you embrac'd him
With too much ardor for a stranger, and
Met him with kisses neyther chaste nor comely:
But learne you to forget him, as I will
Your bounties to him, you will find it safer
Rather to bee vncourtly, then immodest.
   Beau. This prety rag about your necke shews well,
And being coorse and little worth, it speakes you,
As terrible as thrifty.
   Rom. Madam.
   Beau. Yes.
And this strong belt in which you hang your honor
Will out-last twenty scarfs.
   Rom. What meane you, Lady?
   Beau. And all else about you Cap a pe,
So vniforme in spite of handsomnesse,
Shews such a bold contempt of comelinesse,
That tis not strange your Laundresse in the League,
Grew mad with loue of you.
   Rom. Is my free counsayle
Answerd with this ridiculous scorne?
   Beau. These obiects
Stole very much of my attention from me,

Yet

The Fatall Dowry.

Yet something I remember, to speake truth,
Deceyued grauely, but to little purpose,
That almost would haue made me sweare, some Curate
Had stolne into the person of *Romont*,
And in the praise of goodwife honesty,
Had read an homely.

Rom. By thy hand.

Bean. And sword,
I will make vp your oath, twill want weight else.
You are angry with me, and poore I laugh at it.
Do you come from the Campe, which affords onely
The conuersation of cast suburbe whores,
To set downe to a Lady of my ranke,
Lymits of entertainmmen?

Rom. Sure a Legion has possest this woman.

Bean. One stamp more would do well: yet I desire not
You should grow horne-mad, till you haue a wife.
You are come to warme meate, and perhaps cleane linnen:
Feed, weare it, and bee thankfull. For me, know,
That though a thousand watches were set on mee,
And you the Master-spy, I yet would vse,
The liberty that best likes mee. I will reuell,
Feast, kisse, imbreace, perhaps grant larger fauours:
Yet such as liue vpon my meanes, shall know
They must not murmur at it. If my Lord
Bee now growne yellow, and has chose out you
To serue his Iealouzy that way, tell him this,
You haue something to informe him. *Exit Bean.*

Rom. And I will.
Beleeue it wicked one I will. Heare, Heauen,
But hearing pardon mee: if these fruts grow
Vpon the tree of marriage, let me shun it,
As a forbidden sweete. An heyre and rich,
Young, beautifull, yet adde to this a wife,
And I will rather choose a Spittle sinner
Carted an age before, though three parts rotten,
And take it for a blessing, rather then

Bee

The Fatall Dowry.

Be fettered to the hellish slauery
Of such an impudence.
  Enter Baumont with writings.
 Bau. Collonell, good fortune
To meet you thus: you looke sad, but Ile tell you
Something that shall remoue it. Oh how happy
Is my Lord *Charaloys* in his faire bride!
 Rom. A happy man indeede!--pray you in what?
 Bau. I dare sweare, you would thinke so good a Lady,
A dower sufficient.
 Rom. No doubt. But on.
 Bau. So faire, so chaste, so vertuous: so indeed
All that is excellent.
 Rom. Women haue no cunning to gull the world.
 Bau. Yet to all these, my Lord
Her father giues the full addition of
All he does now possesse in *Burgundy*:
These writings to confirme it, are new seal'd
And I most fortunate to present him with them,
I must goe seeke him out, can you direct mee?
 Rom. You'l finde him breaking a young horse.
 Bau. I thanke you.   *Exit Baumont.*
 Rom. I must do something worthy *Charaloys* friendship.
If she were well inclin'd to keepe her so,
Deseru'd not thankes: and yet to stay a woman
Spur'd headlong by hot lust, to her owne ruine,
Is harder then to prop a failing towre
With a deceiuing reed.   *Enter Rochfort.*
 Roch. Some one seeke for me,
As soone as he returnes.
 Rom. Her father! ha?
How if I breake this to him? sure it cannot
Meete with an ill construction. His wisedome
Made powerfull by the authority of a father,
Will warrant and giue priuiledge to his counsailes.
It shall be so--- my Lord.
 Roch. Your friend *Romont*: would you ought with me?
            Rom.

The Fatall Dowry.

Rom. I stand so ingag'd
To your so many fauours, that I hold it
A breach in thankfulnesse, should I not discouer,
Though with some imputation to my selfe,
All doubts that may concerne you.

Roch. The performance
Will make this protestation worth my thanks.

Rom. Then with your patience lend me your attention
For what I must deliuer, whispered onely
You will with too much griefe receiue.

Enter Beaumelle, Bellapert.

Beau. See wench!
Vpon my life as I forespake, hee's now
Preferring his complaint: but be thou perfect,
And we will fit him.

Bell. Feare not me, pox on him:
A Captaine turne Informer against kissing?
Would he were hang'd vp in his rusty Armour:
But if our fresh wits cannot turne the plots
Of such a mouldy murrion on it selfe;
Rich cloathes, choyse fare, and a true friend at a call,
With all the pleasures the night yeelds, forsake vs.

Roch. This in my daughter? doe not wrong her.

Bell. Now begin.
The games afoot, and wee in distance.

Beau. Tis thy fault, foolish girle, pinne on my vaile,
I will not weare those iewels. Am I not
Already matcht beyond my hopes? yet still
You prune and set me forth, as if I were
Againe to please a suyter.

Bell. Tis the course
That our great Ladies take.

Rom. A weake excuse.

Beau. Those that are better seene, in what concernes
A Ladies honour and faire fame, condemne it.
You waite well, in your absence, my Lords friend
The vnderstanding, graue and wise *Romont*,

The Fatall Dowry.

Rom. Must I be still her sport?

Beau. Reproue me for it.
And he has traueld to bring home a iudgement
Not to be contradicted. You will say
My father, that owes more to yeeres then he,
Has brought me vp to musique, language, Courtship,
And I must vse them. True, but not t'offend,
Or render me suspected.

Roch. Does your fine story begin from this?

Beau. I thought a parting kisse
From young *Nouall*, would haue displeas'd no more
Then heretofore it hath done; but I finde
I must restrayne such fauours now; looke therefore
As you are carefull to continue mine,
That I no more be visited. Ile endure
The strictest course of life that iealousie
Can thinke secure enough, ere my behauiour
Shall call my fame in question.

Rom. Ten dissemblers
Are in this subtile deuill. You beleeue this?

Roch. So farre that if you trouble me againe
With a report like this, I shall not onely
Iudge you malicious in your disposition,
But study to repent what I haue done
To such a nature.

Rom. Why, 'tis exceeding well.

Roch. And for you, daughter, off with this, off with it:
I haue that confidence in your goodnesse, I,
That I will not consent to haue you liue
Like to a Recluse in a cloyster: goe
Call in the gallants, let them make you merry,
Vse all fit liberty.

Bell. Blessing on you.
If this new preacher with the sword and feather
Could proue his doctrine for Canonicall,
We should haue a fine world. *Exit Bellapert.*

Roch. Sir, if you please

To

The Fatall Dowry.

To beare your selfe as fits a Gentleman,
The house is at your seruice: but if not,
Though you seeke company else where, your absence
Will not be much lamented—— *Exit Rochfort.*
  Rom. If this be
The recompence of striuing to preserue
A wanton gigglet honest, very shortly
'Twill make all mankinde Panders.——Do you smile,
Good Lady Loosenes? your whole sex is like you,
And that man's mad that seekes to better any:
What new change haue you next?
  Beau. Oh, feare not you, sir,
Ile shift into a thousand, but I will
Conuert your heresie.
  Rom. What heresie? Speake.
  Beau. Of keeping a Lady that is married,
From entertayning seruants.—— *Enter Nouall Iu. Mala-*
O, you are welcome.   *tine, Liladam, Aymer,*
Vse any meanes to vexe him,   *Pontalier.*
And then with welcome follow me.   *Exit Beau.*
  Nou. You are tyr'd
With your graue exhortations, Collonell.
  Lilad. How is it? Fayth, your Lordship may doe well,
To helpe him to some Church-preferment; 'tis
Now the fashion, for men of all conditions,
How euer they haue liu'd, to end that way.
  Aym. That face would doe well in a surplesse.
  Rom. Rogues, be silent——or——
  Pont. S'death will you suffer this?
  Rom. And you, the master Rogue, the coward rascall,
I shall be with you suddenly.
  Nou. Pontallier,
If I should strike him, I know I shall kill him;
And therefore I would haue thee beate him, for
Hee's good for nothing else.
  Lilad. His backe
Appeares to me, as it would tire a Beadle,

G 2   And

The Fatall Dowry.

And then he has a knotted brow, would bruise
A courtlike hand to touch it.
  Aym. Hee lookes like
A Curryer when his hides grown deare.
  Pont. Take heede he curry not some of you.
  Non. Gods me, hee's angry.
  Rom. I breake no lests, but I can breake my sword
About your pates.   *Enter Charaloyes and*
  Lila. Heres more.   *Baumont.*
  Aym. Come let's bee gone,
VVee are beleaguerd.
  Non. Looke they bring vp their troups.
  Pont. Will you sit downe with this disgrace?
You are abus'd most grosely.
  Lila. I grant you, Sir, we are, and you would haue vs
Stay and be more abus'd.
  Non. My Lord, I am sorry,
Your house is so inhospitable, we must quit it.   *Exeunt.*
  Cha. Prethee *Romont*, what caus'd this vprore? *Manent*
  Rom. Nothing.   *Char. Rom.*
They laugh'd and vs'd their scuruy wits vpon mee.
  Char. Come, tis thy Iealous nature: but I wonder
That you which are an honest man and worthy,
Should foster this suspition: no man laughes;
No one can whisper, but thou apprehend'st
His conference and his scorne reflects on thee:
For my part they should scoffe their thin wits out,
So I not heard 'em, beate me, not being there.
Leaue, leaue these fits, to conscious men, to such
As are obnoxious, to those foolish things
As they can gibe at.
  Rom. VVell, Sir.
  Char. Thou art know'n
Valiant without defect, right defin'd,
Which is (as fearing to doe iniury,
As tender to endure it) not a brabbler,
A swearer,

Rom.

The Fatall Dowry.

Rom. Pish, pish, what needs this my Lord?
If I bee knowne none such, how vainly, you
Do cast away good counsaile? I haue lou'd you,
And yet must freely speake: so young a tutor,
Fits not so old a Souldier as I am.
And I must tell you, t'was in your behalfe
I grew inraged thus, yet had rather dye,
Then open the great cause a syllable further.

Cha. In my behalfe? wherein hath *Charalois*
Vnfitly so demean'd himselfe, to giue
The least occasion to the loosest tongue,
To throw aspersions on him, or so weakely
Protected his owne honor, as it should
Need a defence from any but himselfe?
They are fooles that iudge me by my outward seeming,
Why should my gentlenesse beget abuse?
The Lion is not angry that does sleepe,
Nor euery man a Coward that can weepe.
For Gods sake speake the cause.

Rom. Not for the world.
Oh it will strike disease into your bones
Beyond the cure of physicke, drinke your blood,
Rob you of all your rest, contract your sight,
Leaue you no eyes but to see misery,
And of your owne, nor speach but to wish thus
Would I had perish'd in the prisons iawes,
From whence I was redeem'd, twill weare you old,
Before you haue experience in that Art,
That causes your affliction.

Cha. Thou dost strike
A deathfull coldnesse to my harts high heate,
And shrinkst my liuer like the *Calenture*.
Declare this foe of mine, and lifes, that like
A man I may encounter and subdue it,
It shall not haue one such effect in mee,
As thou denouncest: with a Souldiers arme,
If it be strength, Ile meet it: if a fault

G 3   Belonging

The Fatall Dowry.

Belonging to my mind, Ile cut it off
With mine owne reason, as a Scholler should
Speake, though it make mee monstrous.

 Rom. Ile dye first.
Farewell, continue merry, and high Heauen
Keepe your wife chaste.

 Char. Hump, stay and take this wolfe
Out of my brest, that thou hast lodg'd there; or
For euer lose mee.

 Rom. Lose not, Sir, your selfe.
And I will venture——So the dore is fast. *Locke*
Now noble *Charaloys*, collect your selfe, *the dore.*
Summon your spirits, muster all you strength
That can belong to man, sift passion,
From euery veine, and whatsoeuer ensues,
Vpbraid not me heereafter, as the cause of
Iealousy, discontent, slaughter and ruine:
Make me not parent to sinne: you will know
This secret that I burne with.

 Char. Diuell on't,
What should it be? *Romont*, I heare you wish
My wifes continuance of Chastity.

 Rom. There was no hurt in that.

 Cha. Why? do you know a likelyhood or possibility
Vnto the contrarie?

 Rom. I know it not, but doubt it, these the grounds
The seruant of your wife now young *Nouall*,
The sonne vnto your fathers Enemy
(Which aggrauates my presumption the more)
I haue bin warnd of, touching her, nay, seene them
Tye heart to heart, one in anothers armes,
Multiplying kisses, as if they meant
To pose Arithmeticke, or whose eyes would
Bee first burnt out, with gazing on the others.
I saw their mouthes engender, and their palmes
Glew'd, as if Loue had lockt them, their words flow
And melt each others, like two circling flames,

          Where

The Fatall Dowry.

Where chastity, like a Phœnix (me thought) burn'd,
But left the world nor ashes, nor an heire.
Why stand you silent thus? what cold dull flegme,
As if you had no drop of choller mixt
In your whole constitution, thus preuailes,
To fix you now, thus stupid hearing this?

Cha. You did not see 'em on my Couch within,
Like George a horse-backe, on her, nor a bed?

Rom. Noe.

Cha. Ha, ha.

Rom. Laugh yee? eene so did your wife,
And her indulgent father.

Cha. They were wise.
Wouldst ha me be a foole?

Rom. No, but a man.

Cha. There is no dramme of manhood to suspect,
On such thin ayrie circumstance as this
Meere complement and courtship. Was this tale
The hydeous monster which you so conceal'd?
Away, thou curious impertinent
And idle searcher of such leane nice toyes.
Goe, thou sedicious sower of debate:
Fly to such matches, where the bridegroome doubts
He holdes not worth enough to counteruaile
The vertue and the beauty of his wife.
Thou buzzing drone that 'bout my eares dost hum,
To strike thy rankling sting into my heart,
Whose venom, time, nor medicine could asswage.
Thus doe I put thee off, and confident
In mine owne innocency, and desert,
Dare not conceiue her so vnreasonable,
To put *Nouall* in ballance against me,
An vpstart cran'd vp to the height he has.
Hence busiebody, thou'rt no friend to me,
That must be kept to a wiues iniury,

Rom. Ist possible? farewell, fine, honest man,
Sweet temper'd Lord adieu; what Apoplexy

Hath

The Fatall Dowry.

Hath knit fence vp? Is this *Romonts* reward?
Beare witnes the great spirit of my father,
With what a healthfull hope I administer
This potion that hath wrought so virulently,
I not accuse thy wife of act, but would
Preuent her *Præcipuce*, to thy dishonour,
Which now thy tardy sluggishnesse will admit.
Would I had seene thee grau'd with thy great Sire,
Ere liue to haue mens marginall fingers point
At *Charaloys*, as a lamented story.
An Emperour put away his wife for touching
Another man, but thou wouldst haue thine tasted
And keepe her (I thinke.) Puffe. I am a fire
To warme a dead man, that waste out my selfe.
Bleed——what a plague, a vengeance i'st to mee,
If you will be a Cuckold? heere I shew
A swords point to thee, this side you may shun,
Or that; the perrill, if you will runne on,
I cannot helpe it.

  Cha. Didst thou neuer see me
Angry, *Romont*?

  Rom. Yes, and pursue a foe
Like lightening.

  Char. Prethee see me so no more.
I can be so againe. Put vp thy sword,
And take thy selfe away, lest I draw mine.

  Rom. Come fright your foes with this: sir, I am your (friend,
And dare stand by you thus.

  Char. Thou art not my friend,
Or being so, thou art mad, I must not buy
Thy friendship at this rate; had I iust cause,
Thou knowst I durst pursue such iniury
Through fire, ayre, water, earth, nay, were they all
Shuffled againe to *Chaos*, but ther's none.
Thy skill, *Romont*, consists in camps, not courts.
Farewell, vnciuill man, let's meet no more.
Heere our long web of friendship I vntwist.

Shall

The Fatall Dowry.

Shall I goe whine, walke pale, and locke my wife
For nothing, from her births free liberty,
That open'd mine to me? yes; if I doe
The name of cuckold then, dog me with scorne.
I am a *Frenchman*, no *Italian* borne. *Exit.*
Rom. A dull *Dutch* rather: fall and coole (my blood)
Boyle not in zeale of thy friends hurt, so high,
That is so low, and cold himselfe in't. Woman,
How strong art thou, how easily beguild?
How thou dost racke vs by the very hornes?
Now wealth I see change manners and the man:
Something I must do mine owne wrath to asswage,
And note my friendship to an after-age. *Exit.*

Actus quartus.   *Scæna prima.*

Enter Nouall Iunior, as newly dressed, a Taylor, Barber, Perfumer, Liladam, Aymour, Page.

Nou. Mend this a little: pox! thou hast burnt me. oh fie vpon't, O Lard, hee has made me smell (for all the world) like a flaxe, or a red headed womans chamber: powder, powder, powder.

Perf. Oh sweet Lord!   *Nouall sits in a chaire,*
Page. That's his Perfumer.   *Barber orders his haire,*
Tayl. Oh deare Lord,   *Perfumer giues powder,*
Page. That's his Taylor.   *Taylor sets his clothes.*

Nou. Monsieur *Liladam*, & *Aymour*, how allow you the modell of these clothes?

Aym. Admirably, admirably, oh sweet Lord I assuredly it's pitty the wormes should eate thee.

Page. Here's a fine Cell; a Lord, a Taylor, a Perfumer, a Barber, and a paire of *Mounsieurs*: 3 to 3, as little will in the one, as honesty in the other. S'foote ile into the country againe, learne to speake truth, drinke Ale, and conuerse with

H   my

The Fatall Dowry.

my fathers Tenants; here I heare nothing all day, but vpon my soule as I am a Gentleman, and an honest man.

Aym. I vow and affirme, your Taylor must needs be an expert Geometrician, he has the Longitude, Latitude, Altitude, Profundity, euery Demension of your body, so exquisitely, here's a lace layd as directly, as if truth were a Taylor.

Page. That were a miracle.

Lila. With a haire breadth's errour, ther's a shoulder piece cut, and the base of a pickadille in *puncto*.

Aym. You are right, Mounsieur his vestaments fit: as if they grew vpon him, or art had wrought 'em on the same loome, as nature fram'd his Lordship as if your Taylor were deepely read in Astrology, and had taken measure of your honourable body, with a *Iacobs* staffe, an *Ephimerides*.

Tayl. I am bound t'ee Gentlemen.

Page. You are deceiu'd, they'l be bound to you, you must remember to trust 'em none.

Nou. Nay, fayth, thou art a reasonable neat Artificer, giue the diuell his due.

Page. I, if hee would but cut the coate according to the cloth still.

Nou. I now want onely my misters approbation, who is indeed, the most polite punctuall Queene of dressing in all *Burgundy*. Pah, and makes all other young Ladies appeare, as if they came from boord last weeke out of the country, Is't not true, *Liladam* ?

Lila. True my Lord, as if any thing your Lordship could say, could be otherwise then true.

Nou. Nay, a my soule, 'tis so, what fouler obiect in the world, then to see a young faire, handsome beauty, vnhandsomely dighted and incongruently accoutred; or a hopefull *Chevalier*, vnmethodically appointed, in the externall ornaments of nature? For euen as the Index tels vs the contents of stories, and directs to the particular Chapters, euen so

doea

The Fatall Dowry.

does the outward habit and superficiall order of garments (in man & woman) giue vs a tast of the spirit, and demonstratiuely poynt (as it were a manuall note from the margin) all the internall quality, and habiliment of the soule, and there cannot be a more euident, palpable, grosse manifestation of poore degenerate dunghilly blood, and breeding, then rude, vnpolish'd, disordered and slouenly outside.

Page. An admirable lecture. Oh all you gallants, that hope to be saued by your cloathes, edify, edify.

Aym. By the Lard, sweet Lard, thou deseru'st a pension o'the State.

Page. Oth' Taylors, two such Lords were able to spread Taylors ore the face of a whole kingdome.

Nou. Pox a this glasse lit flatters, I could find in my heart to breake it.

Page. O saue the glasse my Lord, and breake their heads, they are the greater flatterers I assure you.

Aym. Flatters, detracts, impayres, yet put it by,
Lest thou deare Lord (*Narcissus*-like) should doate
Vpon thy selfe, and dye; and rob the world
Of natures copy, that she workes forme by.

Lila. Oh that I were the Infanta Queene of Europe,
Who (but thy selfe sweete Lord) shouldst marry me.

Nou. I marry? were there a Queene oth' world, not I.
Wedlocke? no padlocke, horslocke, I weare spurrs   *He*
To keepe it off my heeles; yet my *Aymour,*   *capers.*
Like a free wanton iennet i'th meddows,
I looke about, and neigh, take hedge and ditch,
Feed in my neighbours pastures, picke my choyce
Of all their faire-maind-mares: but married once,
A man is stak'd, or pown'd, and cannot graze
Beyond his owne hedge.

      Enter Pontallier, and Malotin.

Pont. I haue waited, sir,
Three houres to speake w'ee, and not take it well,
Such magpies, are admitted, whilst I daunce
Attendance.

H 2   *Lila.*

The Fatall Dowry.

Lila. Magpies? what d'ee take me for?
Pont. A long thing with a most vnpromising face.
Aym. I'll ne're aske him, what he takes me for.
Mal. Doe not, sir,
For hee'l goe neere to tell you.
Pont. Art not thou a Barber Surgeon?
Barb. Yes sira, why?
Pont. My Lord is sorely troubled with two scabs.
Lila. Aym. Humph——
Pont. I prethee cure him of 'em.
Nou. Pish: no more,
Thy gall sure's ouerthrowne; these are my Councell,
And we were now in serious discourse.
Pont. Of perfume and apparell, can you rise
And spend 5 houres in dressing talke, with these?
Nou. Thou'ldst haue me be a dog: vp, stretch and shake,
And ready for all day.
Pont. Sir, would you be
More curious in preseruing of your honour,
Trim, 'twere more manly. I am come to wake
Your reputation, from this lethargy
You let it sleepe in, to perswade, importune,
Nay, to prouoke you, sir, to call to account
This Collonell *Romont*, for the foule wrong
Which like a burthen, he hath layd on you,
And like a drunken porter, you sleepe vnder.
'Tis all the towne talkes, and beleeue, sir,
If your tough sence persist thus, you are vndone,
Vtterly lost, you will be scornd and baffled
By euery Lacquay; season now your youth,
With one braue thing, and it shall keep the odour
Euen to your death, beyond, and on your Tombe,
Sent like sweet oyles and Frankincense; sir, this life
Which once you sau'd, I ne're since counted mine,
I borrow'd it of you; and now will pay it;
I tender you the seruice of my sword
To beare your challenge, if you'l write, your fate

The Fatall Dowry.

Ile make mine owne: what ere betide you, I
That haue liu'd by you, by your side will dye.

Nou. Ha, ha, would'st ha' me challenge poore *Romont*?
Fight with close breeches, thou mayst thinke I dare not.
Doe not mistake me (cooze) I am very valiant,
But valour shall not make me such an Asse.
What vse is there of valour (now a dayes?)
'Tis sure, or to be kill'd, or to be hang'd.
Fight thou as thy minde moues thee, 'tis thy trade,
Thou hast nothing else to doe; fight with *Romont*?
No, i'le not fight vnder a Lord.

Pont. Farewell, sir, I pitty you.
Such louing Lords walke their dead honours graues,
For no companions fit, but fooles and knaues.
Come *Malotin*.   *Exeunt Pont. Mal.*

Enter Romont.

Lila. 'Sfoot, *Colbran*, the low gyant.

Aym. He has brought a battaile in his face, let's goe.

Page. Colbran d'ee call him? hee'l make some of you smoake, I beleeue.

Rom. By your leaue, sirs.

Aym. Are you a Consort?

Rom. D'ee take me for
A fidler? ya're deceiu'd, looke. Ile pay you.   *Kickes 'em.*

Page. It seemes he knows you one, he bumfiddles you so.

Lila. Was there euer so base a fellow?

Aym. A rascall?

Lila. A most vnciuill Groome?

Aym. Offer to kicke a Gentleman, in a Noblemans chamber? A pox of your manners.

Lila. Let him alone, let him alone, thou shalt lose thy arme, fellow: if wee stirre against thee, hang vs.

Page. S'foote, I thinke they haue the better on him, though they be kickd, they talke so.

Lila. Let's leaue the mad Ape.

Nou. Gentlemen.

Lilad. Nay, my Lord, we will not offer to dishonour you

H 3   so

The Fatall Dowry.

so much as to stay by you, since hee's alone.

Nou. Harke you.

Aym. We doubt the cause, and will not disparage you, so much as to take your Lordships quarrell in hand. Plague on him, how he has crumpled our bands.

Page. Ile eene away with 'em, for this souldier beates man, woman, and child. *Exeunt. Manent Nou. Rom.*

Nou. What meane you, sir? My people.

Rom. Your boye's gone, *Lockes the doore.*
And doore's lockt, yet for no hurt to you,
But priuacy: call vp your blood againe, sir, be not affraid, I do
Beseech you, sir, (and therefore come) without more cir-
Tell me how farre the passages haue gone (cumstance
'Twixt you, and your faire Mistresse *Beaumelle.*
Tell me the truth, and by my hope of Heauen
It neuer shall goe further.

Nou. Tell you why sir?
Are you my confessor?

Rom. I will be your confounder, if you doe not. *Drawes a*
Stirre not, nor spend your voyce. *pocket dag.*

Nou. What will you doe?

Rom. Nothing but lyne your brayne-pan, sir, with lead,
If you not satisfie me suddenly,
I am desperate of my life, and command yours.

Nou. Hold, hold, ile speake. I vow to heauen and you,
Shee's yet vntouch't, more then her face and hands:
I cannot call her innocent; for I yeeld
On my sollicitous wrongs she consented
Where time and place met oportunity
To grant me all requests.

Rom. But may I build on this assurance?

Nou. As vpon your fayth. *Drawes Inkehorne*

Rom. Write this, sir, nay you must, *and paper.*

Nou. Pox of this Gunne.

Rom. Withall, sir, you must sweare, and put your oath
Vnder your hand, (shake not) ne're to frequent
This Ladies company, nor euer send
Token

The Fatall Dowry.

Token, or message, or letter, to incline
This (too much prone already) yeelding Lady.
  Nou. 'Tis done, sir.
  Rom. Let me see, this first is right,
And here you wish a sudden death may light
Vpon your body, and hell take your soule,
If euer more you see her, but by chance,
Much lesse allure her. Now, my Lord, your hand.
  Nou. My hand to this?
  Rom. Your heart else I assure you.
  Nou. Nay, there 'tis.
  Rom. So keepe this last article
Of your fayth giuen, and stead of threatnings, sir,
The seruice of my sword and life is yours:
But not a word of it, 'tis Fairies treasure;
Which but reueal'd, brings on the blabbers, ruine.
Vse your youth better, and this excellent forme (Lordship.
Heauen hath bestowed vpon you. So good morrow to your
  Nou. Good diuell to your rogueship. No man's safer   *Exit.*
Ile haue a Cannon planted in my chamber,
Against such roaring roagues.

      Enter Bellapert.

  Bell. My Lord away
The Coach stayes: now haue your wish, and judge,
If I haue beene forgetfull.
  Nou. Ha?
  Bell. D'ee stand
Humming and hawing now?   *Exit.*
  Nou. Sweete wench, I come.
Hence feare,
I swore, that's all one, my next oath 'ile keepe
That I did meane to breake, and then 'tis quit.
No paine is due to louers periury.
If loue himselfe laugh at it, so will I.   *Exit Nouall.*

   Scæna 2.   *Enter Charalops, Baumont.*
  Bau. I grieue for the distaste, though I haue manners,
                                                                                No:

The Fatall Dowry.

Not to inquire the cause, falne out betweene
Your Lordship and *Romont*.

  Cha. I loue a friend,
So long as he continues in the bounds
Prescrib'd by friendship, but when he vsurpes
Too farre on what is proper to my selfe,
And puts the habit of a Gouernor on,
I must and will preserue my liberty.
But speake of something, else this is a theame
I take no pleasure in: what's this *Aymeire*,
Whose voyce for Song, and excellent knowledge in
The chiefest parts of Musique, you bestow
Such prayses on?

  Bau. He is a Gentleman,
(For so his quality speakes him) well receiu'd
Among our greatest Gallants; but yet holds
His maine dependance from the young Lord *Nouall*:
Some trickes and crotchets he has in his head,
As all Musicians haue, and more of him
I dare not author: but when you haue heard him,
I may presume, your Lordship so will like him,
That you'l hereafter be a friend to Musique.

  Cha. I neuer was an enemy to't, *Baumont*,
Nor yet doe I subscribe to the opinion
Of those old Captaines, that thought nothing musicall,
But cries of yeelding enemies, neighing of horses,
Clashing of armour, lowd shouts, drums, and trumpets:
Nor on the other side in fauour of it,
Affirme the world was made by musicall discord,
Or that the happinesse of our life consists
In a well varied note vpon the Lute:
I loue it to the worth of it, and no further.
But let vs see this wonder.

  Bau. He preuents my calling of him.

  Aym. Let the Coach be brought   *Enter Aymiere.*
To the backe gate, and serue the banquet vp:
My good Lord *Charalois*, I thinke my house

Much

The Fatall Dowry.

Much honor'd in your presence.

Cha. To haue meanes,
To know you better, sir, has brought me hither
A willing visitant, and you'l crowne my welcome
In making me a witnesse to your skill,
Which crediting from others I admire.

Aym. Had I beene one houre sooner made acquainted
With your intent my Lord, you should haue found me
Better prouided: now such as it is,
Pray you grace with your acceptance.

Bau. You are modest.

Aym. Begin the last new ayre.

Cha. Shall we not see them?

Aym. This little distance from the instruments
Will to your eares conuey the harmony
With more delight.   *Cha.* Ile not consent.

Aym. Y'are tedious,
By this meanes shall I with one banquet please
Two companies, those within and these Guls heere.

Song aboue.

Musique and a Song, Beaumelle within——ha, ha, ha.

Cha. How's this? It is my Ladies laugh, most certaine
When I first pleas'd her, in this merry language,
She gaue me thanks.

Bau. How like you this?

Cha. 'Tis rare,
Yet I may be deceiu'd, and should be sorry
Vpon vncertaine suppositions, rashly
To write my selfe in the blacke list of those
I haue declaym'd against, and to *Romont*.

Aym. I would he were well of—perhaps your Lordship
Likes not these sad tunes, I haue a new Song
Set to a lighter note, may please you better;
'Tis cal'd The happy husband.

Cha. Pray sing it.

Song below. At the end of the Song, Beaumelle within.

Beau. Ha, ha, 'tis such a groome.

The Fatall Dowry.

Ca. Doe I heare this, and yet stand doubtfull?   *Exit Chara.*
Aym. Stay, him I am vndone,
And they discouered.
  Bau. Whats the matter?
  Aym. Ah!
That women, when they are well pleas'd, cannot hold,
But must laugh out.   *Enter Nouall Iu. Charalois,*
  Nou. Helpe, saue me, murther, murther.   *Beaumelt,*
  Beau. Vndone foreuer.   *Bellapert.*
  Cha. Oh, my heart!
Hold yet a little ——— doe not hope to scape
By flight, it is impossible: though I might
On all aduantage take thy life, and iustly;
This sword, my fathers sword, that nere was drawne,
But to a noble purpose, shall not now
Doe th' office of a hangman, I reserue it
To right mine honour, not for a reuenge
So poore, that though with thee, it should cut off
Thy family, with all that are allyed
To thee in lust, or basenesse, 'twere still short of
All termes of satisfaction. Draw.
  Nou. I dare not,
I haue already done you too much wrong,
To fight in such a cause.
  Cha. Why, darest thou neyther
Be honest, coward, nor yet valiant, knaue?
In such a cause come doe not shame thy selfe:
Such whose bloods wrongs, or wrong done to themselues
Could neuer heate, are yet in the defence
Of their whores, daring looke on her againe.
You thought her worth the hazard of your soule,
And yet stand doubtfull in her quarrell, to
Venture your body.
  Bau. No, he feares his cloaths, more then his flesh
  Cha. Keepe from me, garde thy life,
Or as thou hast liu'd like a goate, thou shalt
Dye like a sheepe.

The Fatall Dowry.

Nou. Since ther's no remedy   *They fight, Nouall*
Despaire of safety now in me proue courage.   *is slaine.*

  Cha. How soone weak wrong's or'throwne I lend me your
Beare this to the Caroach——come, you haue taught me (hand,
To say you must and shall : I wrong you not,
Y'are but to keepe him company you loue.
Is't done? 'tis well. Raise officers, and take care,
All you can apprehend within the house
May be forth comming. Do I appeare much mou'd?

  Bau. No, sir.

  Cha. My griefes are now, Thus to be borne
Hereafter ile finde time and place to mourne.
                                       Exeunt.

    Scæna 3.   *Enter Romont, Pontalier.*
  Pont. I was bound to seeke you, sir.
  Rom. And had you found me
In any place, but in the streete, I should
Haue done,——not talk'd to you. Are you the Captaine?
The hopefull *Pontalier?* whom I haue seene
Doe in the field such seruice, as then made you
Their enuy that commanded, here at home
To play the parasite to a gilded knaue,
And it may be the Pander.

  Pont. Without this
I come to call you to account, for what
Is past already. I by your example
Of thankfulnesse to the dead Generall
By whom you were rais'd, haue practis'd to be so
To my good Lord *Nouall*, by whom I liue;
Whose least disgrace that is, or may be offred,
With all the hazzard of my life and fortunes,
I will make good on you, or any man,
That has a hand in't; and since you allowe me
A Gentleman and a souldier, there's no doubt
You will except against me. You shall meete
With a faire enemy, you vnderstand
The right I looke for, and must haue.

                                          Rom.

The Fatall Dowry.

Rom. I doe,
And with the next dayes sunne you shall heare from me.
Exeunt.

Scæna 4. Enter Charalois with a casket, Beaumelle, Baumont.

Cha. Pray beare this to my father, at his leasure
He may peruse it: but with your best language
Intreat his instant presence: you haue sworne
Not to reueale what I haue done.

Bau. Nor will I —— but ——

Cha. Doubt me not, by Heauen, I will doe nothing
But what may stand with honour: Pray you leaue me
To my owne thoughts. If this be to me, rise;
I am not worthy the looking on, but onely
To feed contempt and scorne, and that from you
Who with the losse of your faire name haue caus'd it,
Were too much cruelty.

Beau. I dare not moue you
To heare me speake. I know my fault is farre
Beyond qualification, or excuse,
That 'tis not fit for me to hope, or you
To thinke of mercy; onely I presume
To intreate, you would be pleas'd to looke vpon
My sorrow for it, and beleeue, these teares
Are the true children of my griefe and not
A womans cunning.

Cha. Can you *Beaumelle,*
Hauing deceiued so great a trust as mine,
Though I were all credulity, hope againe
To get beleefe? no, no, if you looke on me
With pity or dare practise any meanes
To make my sufferings lesse, or giue iust cause
To all the world, to thinke what I must doe,
Was cal'd vpon by you, vse other waies,
Deny what I haue seene, or iustifie
What you haue done, and as you desperately
Made shipwracke of your fayth to be a whore,
Vse th' armes of such a one, and such defence,
And multiply the sinne, with impudence,

Stand

The Fatall Dowry.

Stand boldly vp, and tell me to my teeth,
You haue done but what's warranted,
By great examples, in all places, where
Women inhabit, vrge your owne deserts,
Or want of me in merit; tell me how,
Your dowre from the low gulfe of pouerty,
Weighd vp my fortunes, to what now they are:
That I was purchas'd by your choyse and practise
To shelter you from shame: that you might sinne
As boldly as securely, that poore men
Are married to those wiues that bring them wealth,
One day their husbands, but obseruers euer:
That when by this prou'd vsage you haue blowne
The fire of my iust vengeance to the height,
I then may kill you: and yet say 'twas done
In heate of blood, and after die my selfe,
To witnesse my repentance.
  Beau. O my fate,
That neuer would consent that I should see,
How worthy thou wert both of loue and duty
Before I lost you; and my misery made
The glasse, in which I now behold your vertue:
While I was good, I was a part of you,
And of two, by the vertuous harmony
Of our faire mindes, made one: but since I wandred
In the forbidden Labyrinth of lust,
What was inseparable, is by me diuided.
With iustice therefore you may cut me off,
And from your memory, wash the remembrance
That ere I was like to some vicious purpose
Within your better iudgement, you repent of
And study to forget.
  Cha. O Beaumelle,
That you can speake so well, and doe so ill!
But you had bin too great a blessing, if
You had continued chast: see how you force me
To this, because mine honour will not yeeld

I 3   That

The Fatall Dowry.

That I againe should loue you.   *Beau.* In this life
It is not fit you should: yet you shall finde,
Though I was bold enough to be a strumpet,
I dare not yet liue one: let those fam'd matrones
That are canoniz'd worthy of our sex,
Transcend me in their sanctity of life,
I yet will equall them in dying nobly,
Ambitious of no honour after life,
But that when I am dead, you will forgiue me.

   Cha. How pity steales vpon me! should I heare her
ten words more, I were lost--one knocks, go in. *Knock*
that to be mercifull should be a sinne.   *within.*
, sir, most welcome. Let me take your cloake, *Exit Beau-*
it not be denyed---here are your robes,   *melle.*
you loue iustice once more put them on: *Enter*
There is a cause to be determind of   *Rochfort.*
That doe's require such an integrity,
As you haue euer vs'd--ile put you to
The tryall of your constancy, and goodnesse:
And looke that you that haue beene Eagle-ey'd
In other mens affaires, proue not a Mole
In what concernes your selfe. Take you your seate:
I will be for you presently.   *Exit.*

   Roch. Angels guard me,
To what strange Tragedy does this destruction
Serue for a Prologue?   *Enter Charalois, with Nonals*
   Cha. So, set it downe before   *body. Beaumelle, Beau-*
The Iudgement seate, and stand you at the bar: *mont.*
For me? I am the accuser.   *Roch.* Nonall slayne,
And *Beaumelle* my daughter in the place
Of one to be arraign'd.
   Cha. O, are you touch'd?
finde that I must take an other course,
eare nothing. I will onely blinde your eyes,
or Iustice should do so, when 'tis to meete
n obiect that may sway her equall doome

                                      From

The Fatall Dowry.

From what it should be aim'd at.——— Good my Lord,
A day of hearing.
 Roch. It is granted, speake——you shall haue iustice.
 Cha. I then here accuse,
Most equall Iudge, the prisoner your faire Daughter.
For whom I owed so much to you: your daughter,
So worthy in her owne parts : and that worth
Set forth by yours, to whose so rare perfections,
Truth witnesse with me, in the place of seruice
I almost pay'd Idolatrous sacrifice
To be a false adultresse.
 Roch. With whom?
 Cha. With this *Nouall* here dead.
 Roch Be wel aduis'd
And ere yon say adultresse againe,
Her fame depending on it, be most sure
That she is one.
 Cha. I tooke them in the act.
I know no proofe beyond it.
 Roch. O my heart.
 Cha. A Iudge should feele no passions.
 Roch. Yet remember
He is a man, and cannot put off nature,
What answere makes the prisoner?
 Beau. I confesse
The fact I am charg'd with, and yeeld my selfe
Most miserably guilty.
 Roch. Heauen take mercy
Vpon your soule then: it must leaue your body.
Now free mine eyes, I dare vnmou'd looke on her,
And fortifie my sentence, with strong reasons.
Since that the politique law prouides that seruants,
To whose care we commit our goods shall die,
If they abuse onr trust : what can you looke for,
To whose charge this most hopefull Lord gaue vp
All hee receiu'd from his braue Ancestors,
Or he could leaue to his posterity ?
His Honour, wicked woman, in whose safety

The Fatall Dowry.

All this lifes ioyes, and comforts were locked vp,
With thy lust, a theefe hath now stolne from him,
And therefore———
   Cha. Stay, iust Iudge, may not what's lost
By her owne fault, (for I am charitable,
And charge her not with many) be forgotten
In her faire life hereafter?
   Roch. Neuer, Sir.
The wrong that's done to the chaste married bed,
Repentant teares can neuer expiate,
And be assured, to pardon such a sinne,
Is an offence as great as to commit it.
   Cha. I may not then forgiue her.
   Roch. Nor she hope it.
Nor can shee wish to liue no sunne shall rise,
But ere it set, shall shew her vgly lust
In a new shape, and euery on more horrid:
Nay, euen those prayers, which with such humble feruor
She seemes to send vp yonder, are beate backe,
And all suites, which her penitence can proffer,
As soone as made, are with contempt throwne
Off all the courts of mercy.   *He kils her.*
   Cha. Let her die then.
Better prepar'd I am. Sure I could not take her,
Nor she accuse her father, as a Iudge
Partiall against her.
   Beau. I approue his sentence,
And kisse the executioner: my lust
Is now run from me in that blood, in which
It was begot and nourished.
   Roch. Is she dead then?
   Cha. Yes, sir, this is her heart blood, is it not?
I thinke it be.
   Roch. And you haue kild her?
   Cha. True, and did it by your doome
   Roch. But I pronounc'd it
As a Iudge onely, and friend to iustice,

                                   And

The Fatall Dowry.

And zealous in defence of your wrong'd honour,
Broke all the tyes of nature: and cast off
The loue and soft affection of a father.
I in your cause, put on a Scarlet robe
Of red died cruelty, but in returne,
You haue aduanc'd for me no flag of mercy:
I look'd on you, as a wrong'd husband, but
You clos'd your eyes against me, as a father.
O *Beaumelle*, my daughter.

  Cha. This is madnesse.

  Roch. Keep from me--could not one good thought rise vp,
To tell you that she was my ages comfort,
Begot by a weake man, and borne a woman,
And could not therefore, but partake of frailety?
Or wherefore did not thankfulnesse step forth,
To vrge my many merits, which I may
Obiect vnto you, since you proue vngratefull,
Flinty-hearted *Charaloys*?

  Cha. Nature does preuaile aboue your vertue.

  Roch. No: it giues me eyes,
To pierce the heart of designe against me.
I finde it now, it was my state was aym'd at,
A nobler match was sought for, and the houres
I liu'd, grew tedious to you: my compassion
Towards you hath rendred me most miserable,
And foolish charity vndone my selfe:
But ther's a Heauen aboue, from whose iust wreake
No mists of policy can hide offendors.   *Enter Nouall se.*

  Nou.se. Force ope the doors--O monster, caniball, with
Lay hold on him, my sonne, my sonne.--O *Rochfort*, Officers.
'Twas you gaue liberty to this bloudy wolfe
To worry all our comforts,——But this is
No time to quarrell; now giue your assistance
For the reuenge.

  Roch. Call it a fitter name——Iustice for innocent blood.

  Cha. Though all conspire
Against that life which I am weary of,

K

The Fatall Dowry.

A little longer yet ile ſtriue to keepe it,
To ſhew in ſpite of malice, and their lawes,
His plea muſt ſpeed that hath an honeſt cauſe. *Exeunt.*

Actus quintus. Scæna prima.

Enter Liladam, Taylor, Officers.

Lila.

WHy 'tis both moſt vnconſcionable, and vntimely
T'arreſt a gallant for his cloaths, before
He has worne them out: beſides you ſayd you ask'd
My name in my Lords bond but for me onely,
And now you'l lay me vp for't. Do not thinke
The taking meaſure of a cuſtomer
By a brace of varlets, though I rather wait
Neuer ſo patiently, will proue a faſhion
Which any Courtier or Ianes of court man
Would follow willingly.

  Tayl. There I beleeue you.
But ſir, I muſt haue preſent moneys, or
Aſſurance to ſecure me, when I ſhall ———
Or I will ſee to your comming forth.

  Lila. Plague on't,
You haue prouided for my enterance in:
That comming forth you talke of, concernes me.
What ſhall I doe? you haue done me a diſgrace
In the arreſt, but more in giuing cauſe
To all the ſtreet, to thinke I cannot ſtand
Without theſe two ſupporters for my armes:
Pray you let them looſe me: for their ſatisfaction
I will not run away.

  Tayl. For theirs you will not,
But for your owne you would; looke to them fellowes.

  Lila. Why doe you call them fellows? doe not wrong
Your

The Fatall Dowry.

Your reputation so, as you are meerely
A Taylor, faythfull, apt to beleeue in Gallants
You are a companion at a ten crowne supper,
For cloth of bodkin, and may with one Larke
Eate vp three manchets, and no man obserue you,
Or call your trade in question for't. But when
You study your debt-booke, and hold correspondence
With officers of the hanger, and leane swordmen,
The learned conclude, the Taylor and Sergeant
In the expression of a knaue are these
To be *Synonima*, Looke therefore to it,
And let vs part in peace, I would be loth
You should vndoe your felfe.

  Tayl. To let you goe   *Enter old Nouall,*
Were the next way.   *and Pontalier.*
But see! heeres your old Lord,
Let him but giue his word I shall be paide,
And you are free.

  Lila. S'lid, I will put him to't:
I can be but denied: or what say you?
His Lordship owing me three times your debt,
If you arrest him at my suite, and let me
Goe run before to see the action entred.
'Twould be a witty iest.

  Tayl. I must haue ernest:
I cannot pay my debts so.

  Pont. Can your Lordship
Imagine, while I liue and weare a sword,
Your sonnes death shall be reueng'd?

  Nou. so. I know not
One reason why you should not doe like others:
I am sure, of all the herd that fed vpon him,
I cannot see in any, now hee's gone,
In pitty or in thankfulnesse one true signe
Of sorrow for him.

  Pont. All his bounties yet
Fell not in such vnthankefull ground: 'tis true

K 2   He

The Fatall Dowry.

He had weakenesses, but such as few are free from,
And though none sooth'd them lesse then I: for now
To say that I foresaw the dangers that
Would rise from cherishing them, were but vntimely.
I yet could wish the iustice that you seeke for
In the reuenge, had bin trusted to me,
And not the vncertaine issue of the lawes;
'Tas rob'd me of a noble testimony
Of what I durst doe for him: but howeuer,
My forfait life redeem'd by him though dead,
Shall doe him seruice.

   Nou.se. As farre as my griefe
Will giue me leaue, I thanke you.

   Lila. Oh my Lord,
Oh my good Lord, deliuer me from these furies.

   Pont. Arrested? This is one of them whose base
And obiect flattery helpt to digge his graue:
He is not worth your pitty, nor my anger.
Goe to the basket and repent.

   Nou.se. Away I onely know now to hate thee deadly:
I will doe nothing for thee.

   Lila. Nor you, Captaine.

   Pont. No, to your trade againe, put off this case,
It may be the discouering what you were,
When your vnfortunate master tooke you vp,
May moue compassion in your creditor,
Confesse the truth.   *Exit Nonall se. Pont.*

   Lila. And now I thinke on't better,
I will, brother, your hand, your hand, sweet brother.
I am of your sect, and my gallantry but a dreame,
Out of which these two fearefull apparitions
Against my will haue wak'd me. This rich sword
Grew suddenly out of a taylors bodkin;
These hangers from my vailes and fees in Hell:
And where as now this beauer sits, full often
A thrifty cape compos'd of broad cloth lists,
Here kin vnto the cushion where I sate

Crosse-

The Fatall Dowry.

Crosse-leg'd, and yet vngartred, hath beene seene,
Our breakefasts famous for the buttred loaues,
I haue with ioy bin oft acquainted with,
And therefore vse a conscience, though it be
Forbidden in our hall towards other men,
To me that as I haue beene, will againe
Be of the brotherhood.

   Offi. I know him now:
He was a prentice to *Le Robe* at *Orleance*. (dead,
   Lila. And from thence brought by my young Lord, now
Vnto *Dijon*, and with him till this houre
Hath bin receiu'd here for a compleate Mounsieur,
Nor wonder at it: for but tythe our gallants,
Euen those of the first ranke, and you will finde
In euery ten, one: peraduenture two,
That smell ranke of the dancing schoole, or fiddle,
The pantofle or pressing yron: but hereafter
Weele talke of this. I will surrender vp
My suites againe: there cannot be much losse,
'Tis but the turning of the lace, with ones
Additions more you know of, and what wants
I will worke out.

   Tayl. Then here our quarrell ends.
The gallant is turn'd Taylor, and all friends. *Exeunt.*

   Scæna 2.   *Enter Romont, Baumont.*
   Rom. You haue them ready.
   Bau. Yes, and they will speake
Their knowledg in this cause, when thou thinkst fit
To haue them cal'd vpon.
   Rom. 'Tis well, and something
I can adde to their euidence, to proue
This braue reuenge, which they would haue cal'd murther,
A noble Iustice.
   Bau. In this you expresse
(The breach by my Lords want of you, new made vp)
A faythfull friend.
   Rom. That friendship's rays'd on sand,

K 3   Which

The Fatall Dowry,

Which euery sudden gust of discontent,
Or flowing of our passions can change,
As if it nere had bin: but doe you know
Who are to sit on him?

   Bau. Mounsieur *Du Croy*
Assisted by *Charmi.*

   Rom. The Aduocate
That pleaded for the Marshalls funerall,
And was checkt for it by *Nouall.*

   Bau. The same.

   Rom. How fortunes that?

   Bau. Why, sir, my Lord *Nouall*
Being the accuser, cannot be the Iudge,
Nor would grieue *Rochfort,* but Lord *Charaloys*
(How-euer he might wrong him by his power,)
Should haue an equall hearing.

   Rom. By my hopes
Of *Charaloys* acquitall, I lament
That reuerent old mans fortune.

   Bau. Had you seene him,
As to my griefe I haue now promis'd patience,
And ere it was beleeu'd, though spake by him
That neuer brake his word, inrag'd againe
So far as to make warre vpon those heires,
Which not a barbarous Scythian durst presume
To touch, but with a superstitious feare,
As something sacred, and then curse his daughter,
But with more frequent violence himselfe,
As if he had bin guilty of her fault,
By being incredulous of your report,
You would not onely iudge him worthy pitty,
But suffer with him.   *Enter Charalois, with*
But heere comes the prisoner,   *Officers.*
I dare not stay to doe my duty to him,
Yet rest assur'd, all possible meanes in me
To doe him seruice, keepes you company.   *Exit Bau.*

   Rom. It is not doubted.

                                Cha

The Fatall Dowry.

Cha. Why, yet as I came hither,
The people apt to mocke calamity,
And tread on the oppress'd, made no hornes at me,
Though they are too familiar: I deserue them.
And knowing what blood my sword hath drunke
In wreake of that disgrace, they yet forbare
To shake their heads, or to reuile me for
A murtherer, they rather all put on
(As for great losses the old *Romans* vs'd)
A generall face of sorrow, waighted on
By a sad murmur breaking through their silence,
And no eye but was readier with a teare
To witnesse 'twas shed for me, then I could
Discerne a face made vp with scorne against me.
Why should I then, though for vnusuall wrongs
I chose vnusuall meanes to right those wrongs,
Condemne my selfe, as ouer-partiall
In my owne cause *Romont?*

Rom. Best friend, well met,
By my hearts loue to you, and ioyne to that,
My thankfulnesse that still liues to the dead,
I looke vpon you now with more true ioy,
Then when I saw you married.

Cha. You haue reason
To giue you warrant for't; my falling off
From such a friendship with the scorne that answered
Your too propheticke counsell, may well moue you
To thinke, your meeting me going to my death,
A fit encounter for that hate which iustly
I haue deseru'd from you.

Rom. Shall I still then
Speake truth, and be ill vnderstood?

Cha. You are not.
I am conscious, I haue wrong'd you, and allow me
Onely a morall man to looke on you,
Whom foolishly I haue abus'd and iniur'd,
Must of necessity be more terrible to me,

Then

The Fatall Dowry.

Then any death the Iudges can pronounce
From the tribunall which I am to plead at.

   Rom. Passion transports you.

   Cha. For what I haue done
To my false Lady, or *Nouall*, I can
Giue some apparent cause: but touching you,
In my defence, childlike, I can say nothing,
But I am sorry for't, a poore satisfaction:
And yet mistake me not: for it is more
Then I will speake, to haue my pardon sign'd
For all I stand accus'd of.

   Rom. You much weaken the strength of your good cause,
Should you but thinke
A man for doing well could entertaine
A pardon, were it offred, you haue giuen
To blinde and slow-pac'd iustice, wings, and eyes
To see and ouertake impieties,
Which from a cold proceeding had receiu'd
Indulgence or protection.

   Cha. Thinke you so?

   Rom. Vpon my soule nor should the blood you chalenge
And tooke to cure your honour, breed more scruple
In your soft conscience, then if your sword
Had bin sheath'd in a Tygre, or she Beare,
That in their bowels would haue made your tombe
To iniure innocence is more then murther:
But when inhumane lusts transforme vs, then
As beasts we are to suffer, not like men
To be lamented. Nor did *Charalois* euer
Performe an act so worthy the applause
Of a full theater of perfect men,
As he hath done in this: the glory got
By ouerthrowing outward enemies,
Since strength and fortune are maine sharers in it,
We cannot but by pieces call our owne:
But when we conquer our intestine foes,
Our passions breed within vs, and of those

The

The Fatall Dowry.

The most rebellious tyrant powerfull loue,
Our reason suffering vs to like no longer
Then the faire obiect being good deserues it,
That's a true victory, which, were great men
Ambitious to atchieue, by your example
Setting no price vpon the breach of fayth,
But losse of life, 'twould fright adultery
Out of their families, and make lust appeare
As lothsome to vs in the first consent,
As when 'tis wayted on by punishment.

Cha. You haue confirm'd me. Who would loue a woman
That might inioy in such a man, a friend?
You haue made me know the iustice of my cause,
And mark't me out the way, how to defend it.

Rom. Continue to that resolution constant,
And you shall, in contempt of their worst malice,
Come off with honour. Heere they come.

Cha. I am ready.

Scæna 3.   *Enter Du Croy, Charmi, Rochfort, Nouall sen.*
            Pontalier, Baumont.

Nou. se. See, equall Iudges, with what confidence
The cruell murtherer stands, as if he would
Outface the Court and Iustice!

Roch. But looke on him,
And you shall finde, for still methinks I doe,
Though guilt hath dide him black, something good in him,
That may perhaps worke with a wiser man
Then I haue beene, againe to set him free
And giue him all he has.

Charmi. This is not well.
I would you had liu'd so, my Lord that I,
Might rather haue continu'd your poore seruant,
Then sit here as your Iudge.

Du Croy. I am sorry for you.

Roch. In no act of my life I haue deseru'd
This injury from the court, that any heere

L   Should

The Fatall Dowry.

Should thus vnciuilly vsurpe on what
Is proper to me only.
   Du Cr. What distaste
Receiues my Lord?
   Rch. You say you are sorry for him:
A griefe in which I must not haue a partner:
'Tis I alone am sorry, that I rays'd
The building of my life for seuenty yeeres
Vpon so sure a ground, that all the vices
Practis'd to ruine man, though brought against me,
Could neuer vndermine, and no way left
To send these gray haires to the graue with sorrow.
Vertue that was my patronesse, betrayd me:
For entring, nay, possessing this young man,
It lent him such a powerfull Maiesty
To grace what ere he vndertooke, that freely
I gaue my selfe vp with my liberty,
To be at his disposing; had his person,
Louely I must confesse, or far fain'd valour,
Or any other seeming good, that yet
Holds a neere neyghbour-hood, with ill wrought on me,
I might haue borne it better: but when goodnesse
And piety it selfe in her best figure
Were brib'd to my destruction, can you blame me,
Though I forget to suffer like a man,
Or rather act a woman?
   Bau. Good my Lord.
   Nou.se. You hinder our proceeding.
   Charmi. And forget
The parts of an accuser.
   Bau. Pray you remember
To vse the temper which to me you promis'd;
   Roch. Angels themselues must breake *Baumont*, that pro-
Beyond the strength and patience of Angels.   (mise
But I haue done, my good Lord, pardon me
A weake old man, and pray adde to that

A

The Fatall Dowry.

A miserable father, yet be carefull
That your compassion of my age, nor his,
Moue you to any thing, that may dis-become
The place on which you sit
   Charmi. Read the Inditement.
   Cha. It shall be needelesse, I my selfe, my Lords,
Will be my owne accuser, and confesse
All they can charge me with, or will I spare
To aggrauate that guilt with circumstance
They seeke to loade me with: onely I pray,
That as for them you will vouchsafe me hearing:
I may not be denide it for my selfe,
When I shall vrge by what vnanswerable reasons
I was compel'd to what I did, which yet
Till you haue taught me better, I repent not.
   Roch. The motion honest.
   Charmi. And 'tis freely granted.
   Cha. Then I confesse my Lords, that I stood bound,
When with my friends, euen hope it selfe had left me
To this mans charity for my liberty,
Nor did his bounty end there, but began:
For after my enlargment, cherishing
The good he did, he made me master of
His onely daughter, and his whole estate:
Great ties of thankfulnesse I must acknowledge,
Could any one freed by you, presse this further?
But yet consider, my most honourd Lords,
If to receiue a fauour, make a seruant,
And benefits are bonds to tie the taker
To the imperious will of him that giues,
Ther's none but slaues will receiue courtesie,
Since they must fetter vs to our dishonours.
Can it be cal'd magnificence in a Prince,
To powre downe riches, with a liberall hand,
Vpon a poore mans wants, if that must bind him
To play the soothing parasite to his vices?
Or any man, because he sau'd my hand,

L 2   Presume

The Fatall Dowry:

Presume my head and heart are at his seruice?
Or did I stand ingag'd to buy my freedome
(When my captiuity was honourable)
By making my selfe here and fame hereafter,
Base slaues to mens scorne and calumnious tongues?
Had his faire daughters mind bin like her feature,
Or for some little blemish I had sought
For my content elsewhere, wasting on others
My body, and her dowry; my forhead then
Deseru'd the brand of base ingratitude:
But if obsequious vsage, and faire warning
To keepe her worth my loue, could preserue her
From being a whore, and yet no cunning one,
So to offend, and yet the fault kept from me?
What should I doe? let any freeborne spirit
Determine truly, if that thankfulnesse,
Choise forme with the whole world giuen for a dowry,
Could strengthen so an honest man with patience,
As with a willing necke to vndergoe
The insupportable yoake of slaue or wittoll.

   Charmi. What proofe haue you she did play false, besides
your oath?

   Cha. Her owne confession to her father.
I aske him for a witnesse.

   Roch. 'Tis most true.
I would not willingly blend my last words
With an vntruth.

   Cha. And then to cleere my selfe,
That his great wealth was not the marke I shot at,
But that I held it, when faire *Beaumelle*
Fell from her vertue, like the fatall gold
Which *Brennus* tooke from *Delphos*, whose possession
Brought with it ruine to himselfe and Army.
Heer's one in Court, *Baumont*, by whom I sent
All graunts and writings backe, which made it mine,
Before his daughter dy'd by his owne sentence,
As freely as vnask'd he gaue it to me.

   Eax. They are here to be seene.

                                                      Charmi.

The Fatall Dowry.

Charmi. Open the casket.
Peruse that deed of gift.
   Rom. Halfe of the danger
Already is discharg'd the other part
As brauely, and you are not onely free,
But crownd with praise for euer.
   Du Croy. 'Tis apparent.
   Charmi. Your state, my Lord, againe is yours.
   Roch. Not mine,
I am not of the world, if it can prosper,
(And yet being iustly got, Ile not examine
Why it should be so fatall) doe you bestow it
On pious vses. Ile goe seeke a graue.
And yet for proofe, I die in peace, your pardon
I aske, and as you grant it me, may Heauen
Your conscience, and these Iudges free you from   *Exit*
What you are charg'd with. So farewell for euer.   *Roch.*
   Nouall se. Ile be mine owne guide. Passion, nor example
Shall be my leaders. I haue lost a sonne,
A sonne, graue Iudges, I require his blood
From his accursed homicide.
   Charmi. What reply you
In your defence for this?
   Cha. I but attended
Your Lordships pleasure. For the fact, as of
The former, I confesse it, but with what
Base wrongs I was vnwillingly drawne to it,
To my few words there are some other proofes
To witnesse this for truth, when I was married:
For there I must begin. The slayne *Nouall*
Was to my wife, in way of our French courtship,
A most deuoted seruant, but yet aym'd at
Nothing but meanes to quench his wanton heate,
His heart being neuer warm'd by lawfull fires
As mine was (Lords:) and though on these presumptions,
Ioyn'd to the hate betweene his house and mine,
I might with opportunity and ease

L 3   Haue

The Fatall Dowry.

Haue found a way for my reuenge, I did not;
But still he had the freedome as before
When all was mine, and told that he abus'd it
With some vnseemely licence, by my friend
My appou'd friend Romont. I gaue no credit
To the reporter, but reprou'd him for it,
As one vncourtly and malicious to him.
What could I more, my Lords? yet after this
He did continue in his first pursute
Hoter then euer, and at length obtaind it;
But how it came to my most certaine kowledge,
For the dignity of the court and my owne honour
I dare not say.

   Nou. se. If all may be beleeu'd
A passionate prisoner speakes, who is so foolish
That durst be wicked, that will appeare guilty?
No, my graue Lords: in his impunity
But giue example vnto iealous men
To cut the throats they hate, and they will neuer
Want matter or pretence for their bad ends.

   Charmi. You must finde other proofes to strengthen these
But meere presumptions.

   Du Croy. Or we shall hardly
Allow your innocence.

   Cha. All your attempts
Shall fall on me, like brittle shafts on armor,
That breake themselues; or like waues against a rocke,
That leaue no signe of their ridiculous fury
But foame and splinters, my innocence like these
Shall stand triumphant, and your malice serue
But for a trumpet to proclaime my conquest;
Nor shall you, though you doe the worst fate can,
How ere condemne, affright an honest man.

   Rom. May it please the Court, I may be heard.

   Nou. se. You come not
To raile againe? but doe, you shall not finde
Another *Rochfort.*

Rom.

The Fatall Dowry.

Rom. In *Nouall* I cannot.
But I come furnished with what will stop
The mouth of his conspiracy against the life
Of innocent *Charaloys*. Doe you know this Character?

Nou.se. Yes, 'tis my sonnes.

Rom. May it please your Lordships, reade it,
And you shall finde there, with what vehemency
He did sollicite *Beaumelle*, how he had got
A promise from her to imoy his wishes,
How after he abiur'd her company,
And yet, but that 'tis fit I spare the dead,
Like a damnd villaine, assoone as recorded,
He brake that oath, to make this manifest.
Produce his bands and hers.

Enter Aymer, Florimell, Bellapert.

Charmi. Haue they tooke their oathes?

Rom. They haue, and rather then indure the racke,
Confesse the time, the meeting, nay the act;
What would you more? onely this matron made
A free discouery to a good end;
And therefore sue to the Court, she may not
Be plac'd in the blacke list of the delinquents.

Pont. I see by this, *Nouals* reuenge needs me,
And I shall doe.

Charmi. 'Tis euident.

Nou.se. That I
Till now was neuer wretched, here's no place
To curse him or my stars.   *Exit Nouall senior.*

Charmi. Lord *Charalois*,
The iniuries you haue sustain'd, appeare
So worthy of the mercy of the Court,
That notwithstanding you haue gone beyond
The letter of the Law, they yet acquit you.

Pont. But in *Nouall*, I doe condemne him thus.

Cha. I am slayne.

Rom. Can I looke on? Oh murderous wretch,
Thy challenge now I answere, so die with him,

Charmi.

The Fatall Dowry.

Charmi. A guard: disarme him.
Rom. I yeeld vp my sword
Vntorc'd. Oh *Charaloys.*
Cha. For shame, *Romont*,
Mourne not for him that dies as he hath liu'd,
Still constant and vnmou'd: what's falne vpon me,
Is by Heauens will, because I made my selfe
A Iudge in my owne cause without their warrant:
But he that lets me know thus much in death,
With all good men forgiue mee.
Pont. I receiue the vengeance, which my loue
Not built on vertue, has made me worthy, worthy of.
Charmi. We are taught
By this sad president, how iust soeuer
Our reasons are to remedy our wrongs,
We are yet to leaue them to their will and power,
That to that purpose haue authority.
For you, *Romont*, although in your excuse
You may plead, what you did, was in reuenge
Of the dishonour done vnto the Court:
Yet since from vs you had not warrant for it,
We banish you the State: for these, they shall,
As they are found guilty, or innocent,
Be set free, or suffer punishment. *Exeunt omnes.*

FINIS.

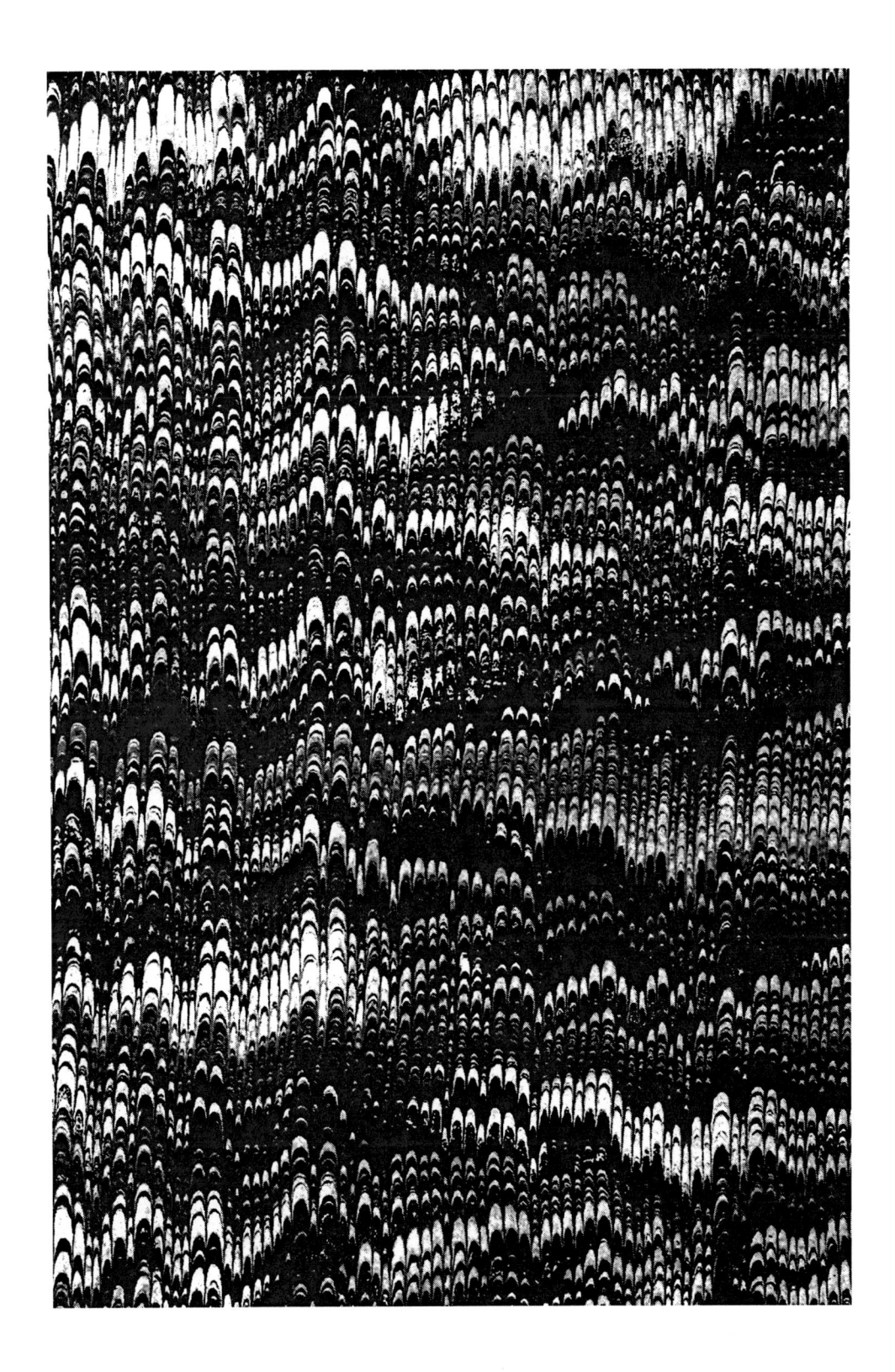

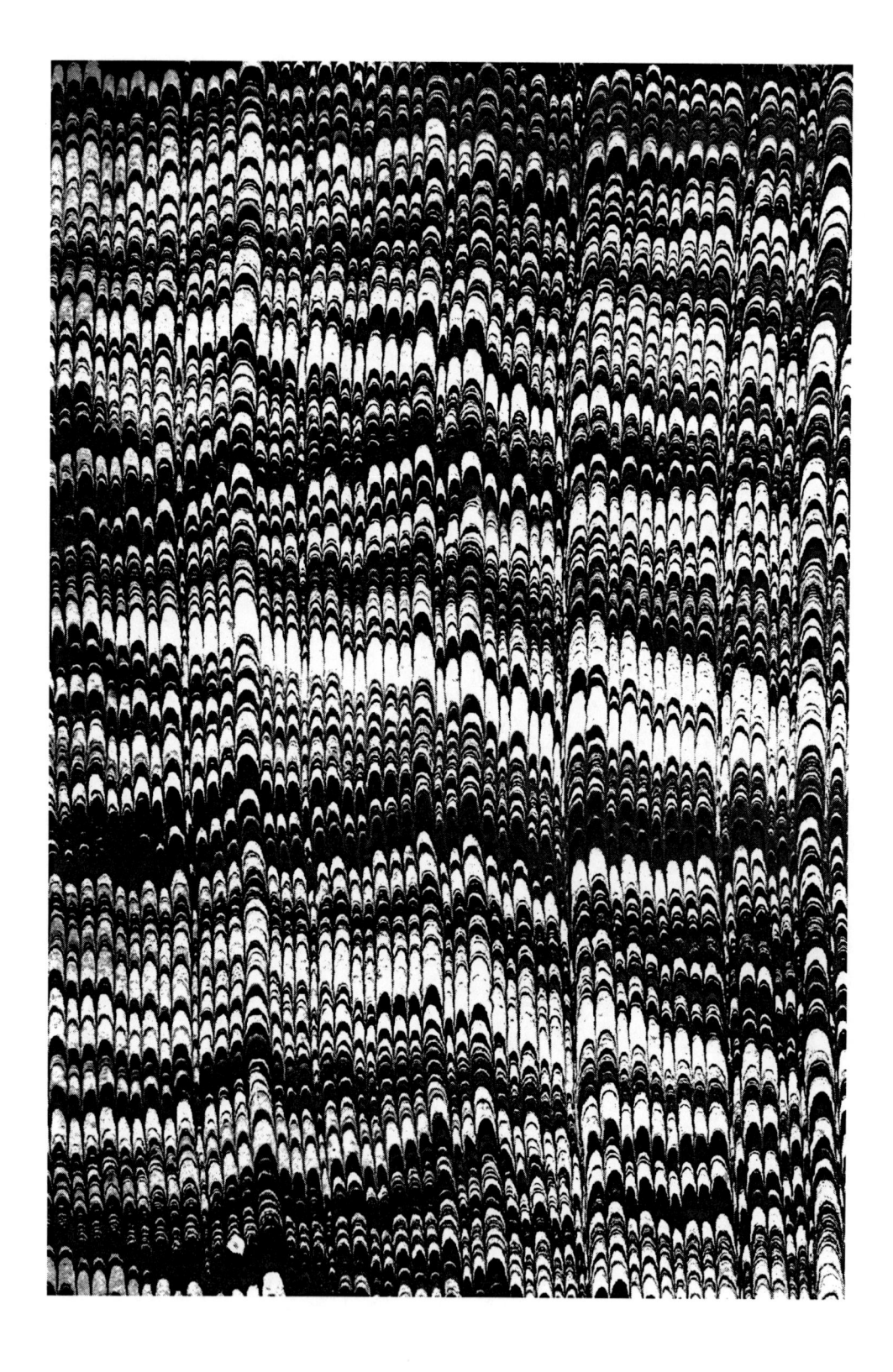

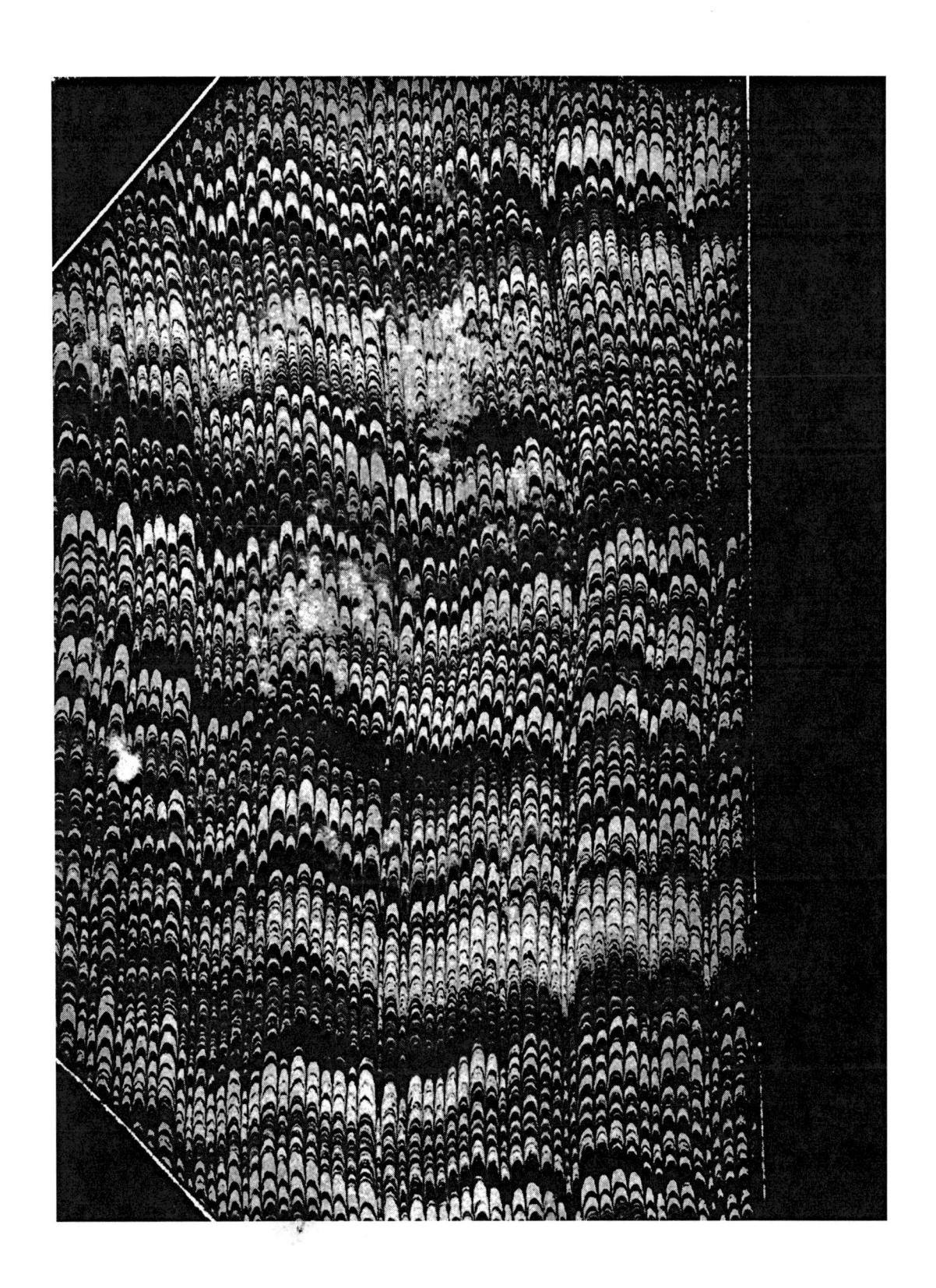